life as Dr Schnorr has done." Teachers, parents, psychologists, and adults hungry for more joy in their lives must read this book.

Dr Mary Harrell, clinical psychologist in private practice in Charlotte, North Carolina and author of *The Mythmaker* and *Imaginal Figures in Everyday Life: Stories from the World Between Matter and Mind*

I0793614

What People Are Saying About

Inside Mindful Teaching

Inside Mindful Teaching provides a unique view of an educator's mental process, both in the moment and in reflection. Written with vulnerability and transparency, it is singular in recounting an experienced teacher's journey of transformation — offering a great gift to all educators. Roberta Schnorr's book is replete with nuggets of gold: the effects of setting intentions, the effect on teaching outcomes of being mindful in preparing, offering, and learning from lessons, the transformation of teachers' lives as well as their teaching produced by regular mindfulness practice, and many more. Familiarity with mindfulness will help readers mine these nuggets but is not essential. Readers will grow their understanding along with the author and her students. If you seek experiential understanding of the power of mindfulness in the transformation of both students and teachers, you will find no better resource than *Inside Mindful Teaching*.
Richard Brady, founder of the Mindfulness in Education Network and author of *Walking the Teacher's Path with Mindfulness: Stories for Reflection and Action*

Inside Mindful Teaching offers a profound exploration of the teaching journey through the lens of mindfulness and intention. The author's reflections on how anxiety, driven by narrow outcomes and expectations, can stifle both the teacher's presence and the students' learning experience are deeply resonant. With honesty and humility, the author shares how developing an awareness of her inner self and fostering a mindful teaching approach transformed her teaching practice — bringing greater clarity, compassion, and presence to the classroom. The wisdom of this book lies

not only in the author's personal evolution but in how these insights are extended to others. By inviting fellow educators to explore mindfulness, the book empowers teachers to be more attuned to their emotional experiences, manage their anxiety, and stay grounded in the face of challenges. It's a call to shift from a model of teaching driven by outcomes to one enriched by awareness, connection, and intentionality. For anyone in education, this book offers both a reflective guide and a source of inspiration, demonstrating that when teachers take the time to care for their own well-being and presence, they create the conditions to nurture the growth of their students as well.
Lorraine Malecki, retired public elementary school principal, New York State

Educators seeking ways to bring mindfulness and reflection into their teaching work – and lives – will find Dr Schnorr's rich stories, and her candid descriptions of her own learning and changes, helpful and encouraging. Readers will find not a how-to manual, but rather the offering of the author's personal quest, filled with obstacles, mentors, discoveries, joy, and peace.
Dr Sharon Kane, Education Professor Emerita and author of *Integrating Literature in the Disciplines and Teaching* and *Reading New Adult Literature in High School and College*

Inside Mindful Teaching is a masterfully crafted account by esteemed Education Professor, Dr Roberta Schnorr. In page after page, Dr Schnorr brings the teachings of Buddhist Zen master Thich Nhat Hanh to her classroom experience as well as to her evolving life. Intimacies, tenderness and gorgeous insights will break your heart wide open with a sense of hope and secrets unearthed. For me, as I read each evocative reflection, intimations opened within me, "Yes, you can do this too. You can bring intention and compassion to your work and

Inside Mindful Teaching

Inside Mindful Teaching

Roberta F. Schnorr

MANTRA BOOKS

London, UK
Washington, DC, USA

CollectiveInk

First published by Mantra Books, 2026
Mantra Books is an imprint of Collective Ink Ltd.,
Unit 11, Shepperton House, 89 Shepperton Road, London, N1 3DF
office@collectiveinkbooks.com
www.collectiveinkbooks.com
www.mantra-books.net

For distributor details and how to order please visit the 'Ordering' section on our website.

Text copyright: Roberta F. Schnorr 2025

ISBN: 978 1 80341 995 4
978 1 78535 265 2 (ebook)
Library of Congress Control Number: 2024951076

All rights reserved. Except for brief quotations in critical articles or reviews, no part of this book may be reproduced in any manner without prior written permission from the publishers.

The rights of Roberta F. Schnorr as author have been asserted in accordance with the Copyright, Designs and Patents Act 1988.

A CIP catalogue record for this book is available from the British Library.

Design: Lapiz Digital Services

UK: Printed and bound by CPI Group (UK) Ltd, Croydon, CR0 4YY
Printed in North America by CPI GPS partners

We operate a distinctive and ethical publishing philosophy in all areas of our business, from our global network of authors to production and worldwide distribution.

Except where noted (specific examples used with permission), the individuals, situations and interactions described in this book are composites based on the author's experiences. All names and identifying details have been changed to protect confidentiality.

Acknowledgements

Many individuals and conditions have supported this book's journey to publication. First, I would like to thank the leaders, editors and staff at Mantra Books (Collective Ink, John Hunt Publishing), for their confidence in, and willingness to support and distribute this work. I also deeply appreciate my editor, Michael, from First Editing, whose exceptional language capacities, keen eye and meaningful suggestions significantly improved the original manuscript.

I must acknowledge the many students, of all ages and perceived abilities, who shared my teaching journey through these years of deep looking into my teaching. All offered many worthy lessons that watered my seeds of intention and insight. Special thanks to Liz, Marisa, Megan, and Rebekah who generously shared details from their own early mindfulness explorations for this text.

Thich Nhat Hanh teaches that our spiritual friends and teachers are not necessarily Buddhist. Before my first steps on my spiritual path, Tom provided significant conditions for my personal healing. I recognize now that he was my first mindfulness teacher. Though he uses different vocabulary, he helped me to touch and begin to transform my pain and to focus on my direct experience — just as it is. This included feeling strong emotions and recognizing my thinking. Much of what I learned was transmitted through his deep, non-judgmental presence, without words. Our collegial conversations about bringing this kind of presence and attention to our teaching encouraged the beginning of my mindful teaching journey.

Readers are invaluable to the writing process. A number of individuals read and responded to various stages of this manuscript. Their feedback was enormously helpful. I offer much appreciation to Pamela Walker, Richard Brady, Joanne

Friday and Thomas Schur for their responses to early versions of this text. And with deep affection, I acknowledge my writing group sisters of over 20 years: Jean Ann, Barbara Beyerbach, Bonita Hampton, Mary Harrell, Sharon Kane, Tania Ramalho, and Christine Walsh. They have accompanied me on every step of this writing process. Their reading, comments, questions and encouragement on so many early pieces and every stage of this manuscript were invaluable. Their writerly lives and their own engaged journeys of transformation and growth continue to inspire me.

The Plum Village community is at the center of this offering. I am so grateful that conditions allowed me to meet Thich Nhat Hanh and receive his wise compassionate teachings in this lifetime. This has been transformational for me, as for so many others whom he has touched. In addition to his books, media and retreats, I have received Thay's energy and teachings through wise and wonderful teachers in the Plum Village tradition who have supported me, and continue to encourage me on this path. I am especially grateful to my mentor, Dharma teacher Joanne Friday, whose love and light guided my very first steps on this path. I also wish to thank Dharma teachers Michael Ciborski, Fern Dorresteyn, JoAnn Rosen, Larry Ward, Peggy Rowe Ward, Richard Brady and Al Lingo who have gifted me and enriched my practice through teaching offerings in many forms.

With sangha all things are possible. I want to share deep appreciation for the various Plum Village sanghas that support me on this path, the foundation of this writing. They, too, are in this book. Let me acknowledge and thank monastic and lay teachers, and sangha siblings from Blue Cliff Monastery, Morning Sun Community, and the Order of Interbeing. I also offer a bow of gratitude to my local Apple Blossom sangha, Blooming Lilac sangha, True Joy of Giving sangha, Cedar Cabin sangha, EMBRACE sangha, and ENVISIONING sangha. You are essential to my practice and my path.

Finally, I thank my daughters, Grete and Molly, who share their offerings in the world with such kindness and deep authenticity. I am touched to see how they are already beautiful continuations of our ancestors. They continually water my seeds of aspiration to transform suffering and to cultivate a generous, compassionate heart.

Contents

For Grete and Molly

and

In honor of Rev. William F. White,
and all of my teaching ancestors

Preface

More than 15 years ago, when I stumbled upon mindfulness practice, there was little support for mindful teaching. In fact, the term *mindfulness* was not yet widely known. Today there are many helpful texts and resources to support teachers who choose this path. This book differs from any others I know in that it focuses on the "inside" story of mindful teaching. I share my inner journey as I stumbled along my beginnings of mindful teaching. I describe some of what I witnessed when I was able (or not) to be mindful throughout various kinds of teaching experiences, including planning, instruction, assessment, feedback, and individual interactions. I reflect on how my observations informed experiments with myself to cultivate my inner conditions as I chose to actively bring mindfulness into the contexts of my teaching work.

Mindfulness is always mindfulness of something. In the pages that follow, I share my exploration of mindfulness of my teaching. I also describe understandings that emerged and the efforts that supported success. I hope these might inform others who wish to investigate their own inner path to foster their capacity for mindful teaching.

By mindfulness, I mean being present and observing what is happening on the outside, as well as my inner experience (i.e., physical sensations, emotions, thoughts), with kind awareness. With awareness, I am learning to bring attention to and accept the realities of my moment-to-moment experience with friendliness and compassion. First, I learned to settle my body. When my body settles, my mind settles. Body and mind can connect as one, both here, now. I become aware of my actual experience in this moment, without judgment. These are the basic conditions of mindfulness for my practice.

Education is complex and multifaceted. For many, across various settings, the work can include some — or even all — of the following:

- long-term and daily planning
- adjusting instruction in the moment
- struggling with student assessments
- working with adult colleagues
- dealing with anxiety before and during instruction
- teaching and interacting with students who are failing our class
- trying to relate to the learners in front of us while managing pain or sadness in our personal life
- learning to communicate skillfully in difficult moments

It includes holding and examining the disappointment when our efforts fall short. Mindfulness helps me grow my capacity to hold it all.

Insights emerged from this multi-year journey. Three conditions are prominent for me in supporting my ability to bring mindfulness to my teaching work: my ability to maintain awareness of, and connection to, my professional knowledge and skills; my inner experience in this moment (i.e., body sensations, emotions, thoughts); and my intention. My intention, which is rooted in my true teacher-self, informed two overarching questions that guide my decisions:

- Who do I aspire to be as a teacher?
- How do I want to impact my students' learning, now and in the future?

My mindful teaching is supported by staying in touch with these conditions, and with my professional knowledge, my changing inner experience, and my intention. Practices for caring for inner experiences and for cultivating my intention intersect to support me during planning and reflection, and during unpredictable moments of instruction, meetings, and other interactions. I can apply practices to shape more skillful thoughts, plans, speech, and actions. Skillful thoughts, plans, speech, and actions are those that are aligned with my intention. Intention also helps me to notice when my decisions and actions are not aligned with my inner teacher-self. With gentle understanding, this disappointment invites and encourages me to learn and adjust, so that I can more often ensure that my teaching offering emerges from my wholeness, from my best teacher-self.

These understandings emerged from my experiences, as I became curious and chose to deepen my exploration. My story is about what came up for me as I tried to remain mindful after the end of my quiet daily meditation period, into the rest of the day. It's about how I tried to maintain that awareness and bring mindfulness to the actual work of teaching. These insights emerged from my successful and unsuccessful explorations, and from listening to beginning teachers talk about their efforts. I also share some comments about mindful teaching experiments from pre-service teachers I taught and supervised in my faculty role in a graduate teacher education program.

As mindfulness became central to my teaching, I experienced unexpected benefits, some of which emerged early in the process. I had renewed energy for my work and clarity about my role and decision making. I developed increased trust in my ability to make difficult decisions and to communicate in trying situations, and I felt this stability not only in my thoughts, but also in my body.

This sense of renewal was, I think, related to my deepening understanding of my self and the wholeness of my capacities, rooted in connection to my inner life. Over the course of my career, I had become so focused on the outer demands of this work that I was often reacting to these without a strong connection to my inner teacher-self. Instead of operating from anxiety about the limitations of the systems I was preparing teachers for, I had a growing sense of agency, and I began to hold desired possibilities less rigidly. While the difficulties of transforming school conditions did not consciously bring me to mindfulness, these connections revealed themselves through my practice and deep looking.

In recent decades, some shifts in educational policies and practices have impacted many of us as teachers. In too many settings, the commodification of schooling can distance teaching from values and leave educators feeling isolated, disempowered and stressed. An over-emphasis on narrowly defined learning outcomes, productivity and competition for resources has caused genuine losses for both students and educators. Differentiation, culturally relevant curricula, rich inquiry learning, collaborative learning, social-emotional learning, and the human needs of students (and adults) are often devalued and are disappearing in many educational settings. The greatest costs are to marginalized learners. In my field of special education, after 20-plus years of progress demonstrating effective practices for inclusive education and meaningful curriculum for the full range of students, we have experienced what feels like a swift reversal toward exclusion and re-segregation. For many students, especially the most complex learners, this has meant a serious loss of learning opportunities.

I recognize now how the anxiety I experienced about this direction in education fueled my focus on preparing the most competent teachers: those most likely to survive and make a meaningful offering, in spite of the difficult conditions. These, I thought, would be teachers who could bring the vision and capacity for transforming educational systems. I realize now that I was missing an essential element.

My mindfulness journey has helped me to view complex change differently. My teacher, Thich Nhat Hanh, developed and birthed Plum Village practices while he and his followers were immersed in the fires of war. His teachings about cultivating peaceful families, organizations and societies, and about healing other complex social issues such as racism and climate change, always emphasized our need to stop, and get in touch first with our own inner suffering. He teaches that transforming ourself is the necessary foundation for bringing the right energy and clarity to individual and collective actions for change on every level.

"Practicing mindfulness in each moment of our daily lives, we can cultivate our own peace. With clarity, determination and patience — the fruits of meditation — we can sustain a life of action and be real instruments of peace." (Nhat Hanh, 1991)

Christiana Figueres, international climate change leader, and a student of Thich Nhat Hanh, expressed it in this way:

> ... intentional cultivating of a mind of love and joy is so critical to our personal resilience, to our personal regeneration, to our personal agency, to our capacity to engage. Without it, there is no capacity to engage in a positive manner, in a constructive manner, in a transformational manner with anything outside ourselves. (Figueres, 2023)

As educators, many of us came to our path wishing to make our best offering to the students who would be part of our journey. But many conditions of our educational institutions (and society) make it difficult to stay connected to the nobility of our work as a precious offering. I believe that for many of us, this direction of changing conditions in educational communities has disconnected us from our source.

Mindfulness helps me begin to find my way back to balance and wholeness to revive the spirit of my teaching. The power of this teaching path flows from the inside. Mindfulness reawakens this inner energy of my aspiration and can help me to sustain my connection to it. It can guide my best decisions, large and small, in times of reflection and planning, and in the moment. Mindfulness helps me to remember who I am at the heart of my teacher-self, and how I aspire to make my offering. This can support me, in difficult conditions, to know the meaning I bring to my teaching. This is the first step; my individual reawakening and transformation is the foundation I need to gain clarity about how I might contribute to changing limiting outer conditions.

My professional work and examples shared in this book may differ from your teaching roles, curricula, students, and contexts. I don't believe that matters. Our inner teaching lives have plenty in common. First, I believe that most of us choose teaching based on a noble intention to be of benefit to our students. Second, my experience has convinced me that, as long as we are solid and engaged in our field, and professionally prepared for our role, where or who or what we teach is irrelevant to the process of developing a mindful teaching practice.

What is clear to me now is that mindful teaching is an inside job. I believe we all have the capacity to bring increasing mindfulness to our teaching. As someone whose life's work was teaching, I want to share my story with you, my fellow educators. These practices can have a profound impact on our teaching, though they are not specific to education. This book emerged from exploring my practice as an educator, with school-age children who had challenging learning characteristics, and with adult graduate school learners who were in a rigorous professional preparation program. The fundamentals of my mindful teaching practice were the same across learners and settings. Perhaps my insights about conditions that support my ability to bring mindfulness to teaching are relevant to other educators, in other settings. My primary wish is that these stories be of benefit, whether you teach college physics or kindergarten, whether your classroom is in a public school, a university, a community space, or a prison.

Key Terms

In the following discussion, I use certain terms in slightly idiosyncratic ways, to designate concepts central to the topics being explored. The following definitions clarify the sense in which they are intended.

Allow – By *allow* I mean trying to *be with* an *inner* experience that may be unfamiliar or challenging, (e.g., physical, emotional) without resistance or judgment. Allowing the non-preferred or unfamiliar inner experience invites me to choose to tune in and observe what is going on for me, in a moment when I might typically disconnect from it. (I hesitate to describe this as *tolerating*, which for me, implies a judgment that it is a negative experience. Central to what I am referring to is the suspension of such judgment, to allow the experience to present itself on its own terms, rather than according to my preconceptions.)

Experiment – Choosing to experiment with myself in a familiar role or context invites me to try something with a different mental and energetic orientation, where I am not focused on control or shaping an experience. It supports my effort to engage differently in a situation or to choose a new response (for me) even though I don't know how it may go. Where *allowing* is about noticing my inner experience, *experimenting* is about outer engagement: a choice of action (including non-action) that is different from my habitual patterns. For example, I would often focus excessively on control and over-plan; I carefully executed steps to try to steer a particular process and outcome. When I choose to experiment with something, I am entering the process with far less control, without attachment to how each step will go, or to a desired outcome. I try to let go of the ways I might typically steer things to go in a desired way. There is space for curiosity. I try to trust my ability to respond flexibly to what may arise and to be open to what might emerge.

Explorations – This is closely related to my description of experiments, but I am referring to a broader, more sustained process. For example, I would refer to a new way of facilitating my class or revising my syllabus with a mindful orientation as an experiment. Whereas I consider this ongoing, multi-year focus on bringing mindfulness to my teaching work as an exploration. My exploration is made up of ongoing experiments related to, in this case, mindful teaching.

Intention – In chapter nine, as I discuss major insights, I provide an expanded explanation of what I mean by intention for my engagement specific to mindful teaching. When I refer to intention more generally in earlier chapters, I mean that I have a particular vision for myself in a role or context (e.g., teacher, parent). Intention is my effort to be conscious of my vision and to try to make decisions and take actions that align with this vision.

Part One

Inner Explorations

Part one (chapters one through four) describes the very unplanned beginnings of my personal mindfulness practice, and how it began showing up unexpectedly in my teaching life. I include several encounters during consulting work with students who have complex disabilities. These reflect how, over time, I became increasingly aware of my inner life while teaching, and the influence of emerging mindfulness practice on my professional work.

Chapter 1

Opening to Mindfulness

Here's how it started for me. I was, quite simply, falling apart. I had no intention of trying out meditation, let alone exploring mindful teaching. Let me describe some of the conditions that introduced me to a mindful orientation to my life, then grew into a personal practice. Later this practice unexpectedly began to infiltrate some of my teaching, creating effects that I could not ignore. Since I was not intentionally pursuing mindful teaching, it took a while for me to understand what was going on.

My Intro to Mindfulness: No Mud, No Lotus (Nhat Hanh, 2014)

This book is about teaching, so in this chapter I provide a brief summary of how I first came to mindfulness, focusing on the important conditions that preceded my accidental beginnings with mindful teaching. Possibilities abound for circumstances that might prompt any of us to stop and examine our life and direction from a new place of inner awareness. The beginning of each person's journey is uniquely his or hers. Mine went like this.

It began with the breakdown. It was like nothing I had ever experienced, even for a moment. My tendency was to operate from an energetic state of over-confidence. I experienced some harshness in my early years, and I learned to "armor up" and always present as strong and in control. Unexpectedly, old trauma that I had buried deep inside was triggered. Everything began to unravel as I experienced a serious mental / emotional breakdown. (And this thing that was triggered was not even the root of the pain. Much more would emerge as I sought understanding and transformation through years of work and practice.)

Though I was unaware, for decades my life had been all about action and busy-ness, creating identities from multiple roles as I hurtled along. As a professional, I brought intellect and skill and a strong work ethic. In these spheres, I was considered productive and high achieving. I was often bold, opinionated, and intense. (Some might say that I was sometimes scary.) The unknown, unacknowledged anxiety that had me constantly spinning and producing to create a worthy identity and to deny vulnerability finally broke through.

A deep depression ensued. Later, after several years of deep exploration and healing with a skilled therapist, I realized that I was one of the lucky ones. I got to wake up, drop the roles and the stories about who I thought I was "supposed to be." I learned to be myself, deciding each day to live from a place of authenticity. This was indeed a conscious choice, and it frightened me. I knew that if I chose this path and let go of my old patterns, I would have to commit fully, across all of my life spheres — family, work, and especially, self. There would be no turning back. There is no such thing as a part-time authentic life.

The work with my therapist James (pseudonym) was a huge relief, and consistently difficult. I remained engaged with parenting and teaching, though for several years I cut back on any extra responsibilities. The process meant paying attention, noticing my experience, learning to recognize and manage anxiety's reactivity and to develop new authentic patterns. I practiced choosing my responses based on *my* vision and intentions, as a daughter, as a mother, as a spouse, as a sister, and as a friend. James helped me to notice when I was viewing experiences through the lens of "other-focus" rather than "self-focus." This orientation was the foundation of my emerging inner awareness, honoring my experience instead of falling into old roles based on what I thought others wanted or expected. Later I would learn how this time of practice reflected the Buddha's simple but profound teaching, "Trust your experience."

I recognized how my therapy process was similar to qualitative research methods I had applied for inquiry into educational settings, looking deeply into the unspoken codes structuring the activity of people within organizations. Now the focus was on studying my "self" and my experience within various systems, including my family and my work. I engaged quickly and deeply with exploring these new understandings, first intellectually, and then, over time, with my whole being, noticing, feeling, and owning my emotional experiences. Early on, as I became able to allow in some realities of my childhood experiences, I was filled with awareness, confusion, anger, and then deep sadness. Talking about these for the first time in therapy helped. I also continued to listen to and revisit family stories and to ask my parents about their life experiences. This was part of my deep looking, which helped me to eventually learn about many conditions in my parents' and ancestors' lives.

Language helped. My therapist invited me to view this self-focus (mindfulness) as an "experiment." My approach was to slow down and begin to try out intuitive (authentic) ways of being in various situations — to notice what unfolded for me, and how others responded. James called this ongoing experiment my "practice," and indeed, the process took a lot of practice. When I occasionally became discouraged and whined about the difficulty, he would remind me, "That's why we call it 'work'." James continually challenged my perceptions of my identity as a separate self, whose power, successes, or failures were mine as an individual. He highlighted my connection to others in the many systems in which I operated. He encouraged me to trust *my* experience and acknowledged the paradox of how well things went when I let go of patterns based on values from the broader culture. For example, my hyper-performance at work and in relationships was sometimes rewarded by others. But this pattern was also very costly to me and to my close relationships. James listened deeply and encouraged me when

I reported experiments that made me feel deeply vulnerable, experiencing a new tender connection to myself and others. He never criticized my habit of presenting with a false sense of power that tried to control people or outcomes. But after stories where I could allow my vulnerability, he would smile, and encourage more experiments in this direction, suggesting, "...and then, you may really be powerful."

But the most important gift I received in my therapy with James was about the transformative power of human presence. This was my first experience with a person who was fully present to me as a human being. He conveyed no expectations or judgments; nothing depending on my performance or skills. For years I had relied on my competence to construct a self that others might see as worthy. In these sessions, I began to drop that version of who I was and explore who I was when I was just *being* without doing or performing. Though scary at first, I began to leave feeling settled, and to trust there was more to who I really was. This encouraged me to continue to try on this other way of being in my life in other relationships — with my family, my friends, and my students.

Within six months of starting therapy, I stumbled upon the book *When Things Fall Apart*, by Pema Chodron (1997). The title instantly resonated with all of my current experience. What she proposed was completely antithetical to everything I had received from my culture. In fact, she sounded a lot like James. As I read and re-read sections, it made sense on a gut level. I found it settling. But Chodron was clear that I was not going to be able to "grow up" unless I took the leap and committed to meditation. Change was not going to come from reading or thinking. The way to tame the confused mind was to sit, daily. So I began to do so, first for 5, then 10 minutes each morning, until I could sit for 20 or 30 minutes in stillness, following my breath, letting go of thinking and returning to the breath again and again.

Within just a few weeks, I began to notice changes. I was emotionally and physically calmer for more moments on many days. I was aware that this new sense of calm was something I had not ever realized was missing from my experience. There were times I did not react immediately to triggers that would typically send me into anger or defensiveness. When I did react, I recognized my patterns and recovered more quickly. I was becoming aware of my inner experience. Mostly because meditation was helping me to manage daily fear and anxiety, I kept it up. I also sought out more books, first by Chodron, and then other meditation teachers. This reading continued to challenge my internalized cultural beliefs and to support my new ways of viewing and being with my experience.

I also began attending yoga classes for the first time at a local yoga center. The integrity of this center's leaders was apparent in all aspects of their business. Each class began with a few minutes of silent meditation, followed by gentle instruction by teachers whose presence was apparent. Like my therapist and Buddhist authors, my yoga teachers also challenged common cultural beliefs and encouraged a focus on allowing all of one's experience, without judgment. For months, tears leaked out during many classes, for no reason I could discern. It was here, I believe, that I was able to begin to feel and transform some of the trauma that my body had held for decades. I experienced deep settling in my body and started to connect with a sense of inner and outer well-being. Yoga was also my introduction to generating and sharing mindful energy in group practice.

During this time, writing became part of my mindfulness practice. I had been engaged in many kinds of professional writing for 20 years. In the midst of the first year of these personal challenges, I was granted a sabbatical to pursue a research and professional development project. At that time, I joined a writing group — eight women colleagues who met monthly to read one another's writing and to offer feedback and suggestions. A structure emerged over time. We took turns hosting monthly meetings in our homes. The first hour was for a potluck meal and conversation. This was followed by three hours to discuss writing, giving our full attention to one piece, one writer at a time. Over time, the genres of shared writing diversified. There were drafts of book chapters, journal articles, conference proposals, reports, and books. Later, there were also poems, personal memoir pieces, and reflections. Our writing group became a safe place where we could share with one another from the heart through our writing, knowing our readers would hold the space and honor the writer, as well as the writing.

I began to write privately about some of my deep wounds from my youth as a way to hold and acknowledge these between my therapy sessions. I pieced together revised understandings about my family, connecting people and events from the long family narrative. As I actively cultivated my own presence with my daughters, parents, students, and others, I began to witness powerful, unexpected responses and very real moments of authentic connection. I often felt compelled to get these stories down, to document what seemed like profound shifts in my way of being in my life. Chapter two is an example of such writing: a story that insisted on being recorded, after my experience with Damien, a 12-year-old student I met on a consultation trip.

Eventually, I decided to share some of my personal writing reflections with my writing group. Writing group became a place where more of my real self could come out. I could present stories of my vulnerability. My personal writing pieces allowed me to invite key others to bear witness to these parts of myself, and to my story as well. The first time I shared a piece of writing that engaged with deeply shameful, painful psychic content, it was received with loving attention and reverence. The next day, I wrote to my writing sisters, acknowledging how they impacted my writing practice:

> Had I not been a member of this writing group, I would not have been writing at all about my experiences through this difficult period. So, while you may think you were not with me, or supportive of me through these dark months, of course you were. You were the ones who modeled and encouraged and taught me, that whatever life brings, "You could write about it." Each time I sat here at my computer or pulled my pen and notebook from my bag at the coffee shop, to feel, to think, to wonder — confused or scared or angry or sobbing — you were all right there, whispering, "Write about it."

The act of writing slowed me down. I could look deeply at what was presenting inside, to feel what arose, and stay with the experience. I would often re-read my pieces, to reconnect with my tender heart, to witness bodily sensations, and to practice my way back to feeling as a way of knowing. In my writing group, I continue to experience first-hand how our shared texts create a context for presence, for risk taking, for deep listening, and for true connection.

Committing

After my therapy ended, I continued to practice meditation and yoga, and to read texts by many Buddhist authors, mostly Western lay teachers. Eventually it was a Vietnamese monk, Thich Nhat Hanh, and his prolific writing about the power of mindfulness, that resonated most strongly with me and became my path. Nhat Hanh (known by his students as Thay, pronounced "Tie") offers accessible and powerful practices for real life. These evolved from a lifetime of his own deep suffering and transformation, especially living through the chaos of two wars in Vietnam. A lifelong peace activist, he was both gentle and fierce, reminding us that we can transform our suffering and our unskillful states of mind. A globally revered Buddhist

Zen master and scholar, he assured us that mindfulness is for everyone; we need not be a Buddhist to benefit.

I began to practice and attend retreats in Thay's Plum Village tradition. Twice I attended retreats led by Thay and supported by large groups of his monastics. Receiving teachings through his daily talks felt personal, even among a thousand other retreatants. His deep presence and energy of compassion were palpable. Thay's teaching went beyond words. In every moment, he embodied mindfulness – walking across the platform; writing notes on the whiteboard; carefully erasing; taking steps as he led a huge throng into the woods for walking meditation; his face slowly breaking into a huge smile; sipping his tea in silence in the midst of hundreds. Every word, every movement, every step, every sip – he was right there, in the here and the now. I not only saw but felt the power of mindfulness and compassion as I gazed in awe. Years later I would understand the energetic experience of these retreats as profound moments of what Thay calls interbeing, our very real connection to one another and more.

As my practice deepened, I realized there could be no real separation between my personal and professional selves. Both continued to grow in response to countless elements within and outside of myself. I recognized how I had been strongly conditioned by many influences, including values and beliefs of the broader culture. Because I was benefiting from mindfulness practice, I sought more wholesome influences to support my new direction, including texts, recorded talks, and retreats. I helped start a local sangha, with several friends from our first retreat. In canonical Buddhist texts, "the sangha" refers to the community of practitioners, with an emphasis on the pivotal role it plays in providing support along the path. Thay's Plum Village tradition encourages all practitioners to join (or create) sangha groups with other practitioners near them. Most sanghas meet weekly to learn and practice together and share how we try to apply teachings to life's wonders and challenges. I received transmission of the Five Mindfulness Trainings, the Buddhist precepts, lovingly translated by Thay and the community. Later, with the skillful guidance of Dharma Teacher, Joanne Friday, I completed my aspirancy and received transmission of the Fourteen Mindfulness Trainings of the Order of Interbeing, to support my intention to assist others on the path.

One is not required to commit to a spiritual tradition or lineage to develop capacities for mindful teaching. I share this part of my experience because being part of this spiritual community significantly enhances and supports my ability to continue to cultivate mindfulness in my teaching and in my life. Let me offer a perspective on how my practice in this tradition may be represented in some parts of this text. I am a student of Zen master Thich Nhat Hanh, and I continue to study and practice in the Plum Village lineage. More than a few of the references to my spiritual practice reflect my understandings and applications both before, and during some very early stages of my practice on this path. I offer my experiences with humility as an individual mindfulness practitioner. I am not a Buddhist scholar or a Plum Village teacher. I am certain that some of what I share may be limited and undeveloped in my interpretations of the teachings that I have received. Please consider my offering with this understanding.

Throughout these early stages of therapy, meditation and yoga practice, and writing, I continued to teach. After the first couple of years, I began once more to accept occasional consultation work, beyond my college teaching role. It was during a challenging and focused consultation visit that my teaching was first disrupted by my evolving mindfulness. In the following chapters, you will read about that — and the rest of my mindful teaching story.

Here's a preview of what is to come in the pages that follow:

Part One: Inner Explorations (chapters two through four) describes several encounters during consulting work with students who have complex disabilities. These reflect how, over time, I became aware of my inner life while teaching, and the influence of emerging mindfulness practice on my professional work.

Chapter two describes an unplanned encounter with a 12-year-old student, Damien, which became my first literacy exploration with a student with significant disabilities (autism, no verbal communication). While I knew something unique had happened for me — and, it appeared, for Damien — it took a long time for me to make sense of this experience.

Chapter three describes my very first attempt to intentionally facilitate a similar exploration with 8-year-old Misha, and how lessons from that unsuccessful effort informed new understandings of essential elements for mindful teaching.

Chapter four describes my time with another student, Keira, and how, with her, I was able to incorporate mindfulness lessons from Damien and Misha with much more intention and skill.

Part Two: Engaged Teaching (chapters five and six) reports and reflects on my experience bringing these new understandings about mindfulness into my work in teacher preparation over several years. It describes the dance between my changing inner experience and my actions, as I took the leap to make mindfulness central to all of my teaching life. These chapters offer a glimpse into early stages of intentional changes in planning and instruction, as I became more present and open in my teaching with adult learners who were professional education candidates.

Chapter five describes my fear and internal struggle as I committed to a full-scale experiment with myself to transform my teaching practice to one grounded in mindfulness.

Chapter six reminds readers that mindful teaching is not all bliss. I describe some of my challenges and missteps, and how mindfulness practices informed my understandings as I attempted new ways of responding.

Part Three: Insights – Conditions that Support Mindfulness in My Teaching Work (chapters seven through nine), identifies and unpacks major lessons I received from my multi-year exploration.

Chapter seven discusses the importance of cultivating and staying connected to my professional knowledge, and how this supports mindfulness in my work as an educator.

Chapter eight discusses how practicing to be in touch with my inner experiences (body sensations, emotions and thoughts) and cultivating skillful responses to these, is also an important condition for my mindfulness in this work.

Chapter nine describes deep understandings that evolved for me about what I call my "intention" in mindful teaching, and how I practice to grow and sustain it.

Part Four: Mindful teaching: learning with and from teacher candidates (chapters ten and eleven) describes how I began to share mindfulness practices with my graduate student candidates. This includes how, over time, I invited them to explore mindfulness in their teaching during field experiences that were part of our shared work.

Chapter ten describes how I invited my pre-service teacher candidates' initial explorations to bring mindfulness to their part-time field experiences, and how this evolved over several years after I had a well-established practice. I offer examples reported by candidates about how some of their experiments went beyond their individual practice to applying mindfulness to their teaching in part-time and then full-time roles in public schools that were part of their graduate studies.

Chapter eleven examines written mindfulness reflections from candidates to learn if the major insights that emerged in my explorations (described in chapters seven through nine) were present in what they wrote and said about their experiences.

Chapter twelve, the conclusion, offers reflections on my journey, including some profound lessons from a few of my teacher candidates who joined me for this exploration of mindful teaching.

I invite you to take in my stories with your heart as well as your mind. I trust you will recognize a "felt" sense of knowing for any parts of my journey that might be of benefit to yours.

Chapter 2

Mindful Teaching 101: Reading and Writing with Damien

Introduction

In this chapter, you will meet Damien, who was a most important teacher for me. It was a teaching experience with Damien that demanded I look deeply into how my emerging personal vulnerability and mindfulness were connected to my capacity to share my best teaching.

My exploration of mindfulness as a critical element of my professional decision making "in the moment" began quite unexpectedly. I was engaged in multi-day consultation with a large school district that was located a long distance from my home. It was an unusual role for me. I was observing practice in programs that served students who were identified as having developmental disabilities, including significant intellectual disabilities. The district had been providing focused professional development to improve practice for programs that served students with these characteristics. Hired as a professional with expertise in best practices, my role was to observe some sample classrooms for one day each and provide a report on impressions of current educational programs for students with intensive learning needs. While on site, I was also expected to provide technical assistance and on-the-spot consultation to teachers for one or two students who presented the greatest challenges.

I had brought my laptop, which had some digital texts and software tools for potential literacy activities, to possibly experiment with students and to share with teachers, as appropriate. I also brought a few resources related to positive behavior supports to engage in assessing and planning with teachers and other team members, if needed.

I would spend each day in a different school and classroom. Before the trip, each teacher had identified a student or two for more focused consultation. At the end of the day, we would meet to discuss feedback and further possibilities for general program issues and / or recommendations for the students identified.

These unusual consultation conditions produced significant anxiety for me. The long travel had been difficult, and I was feeling physically sub-par. I was exhausted, not sleeping well, and unable to eat much. Anxious thoughts would emerge frequently. What might today's class be like? What if the teacher did not want to be observed or work with a consultant? What if my efforts to engage or support a challenging student did not work (in view of the team of adults)? What if my interactions escalated a student's problem behaviors? What if I didn't know what to try or suggest? What would teachers and my district guide think of me if my contributions were not helpful? Of course, these vulnerable states were rarely observable to others. But these internal thoughts and feelings, and my physical limitations, were a very real part of my experience on this trip.

I had been implementing a daily mindfulness practice on my own for about two years prior to this experience. I meditated daily, read from books by meditation teachers each day, and listened to recorded talks by such teachers while driving, or sometimes during household chores. In an effort to manage my escalating anxiety and physical discomfort on this trip, I spent each morning engaged in sitting meditation, walking meditation, reading, and listening to talks. Because I woke up too early and couldn't eat much, I had extra time to practice in my room each morning while awaiting my driver. The morning I made the school visit to Damien's class, I had been very focused with walking meditation and listening to a long talk for one or two hours. Though the anxiety was still there, my body was a bit calmer, and I was able to let go of negative thinking by the time my driver arrived. I was present in my experience, including the uncomfortable parts, but these were no longer overwhelming me. It was time to show up, try to pay attention, and offer whatever I could.

In the following pages I will describe my experience in this day's classroom, most of which focused on one student, Damien. In an email prior to my trip, this teacher had requested that I offer recommendations for Damien, a student who presented frequent challenging behaviors. She described Damien as having "low functioning autism," and indicated that he did not speak, but used a few signs for some communication. She wondered, *"How can I respond to aggressive behaviors from Damien? How do I provide adequate consequences to match his cognitive abilities?"*

A Day with Damien

Another day, another class, another school; I am comfortable with this piece. I feel at home in classrooms. I am curious about the teacher and the students I will meet today. Peter, a special education supervisor from the district office, accompanies me today. The school is structurally odd and fragmented. It is a one-story building with several wings. We go down a hall and then exit. There are a number of other buildings, some are what we called "portables," meaning they are trailers. Of course, the special education class is in one of these "out buildings." Today's teacher is Emily. She has been teaching for three years. She has ten students who are 10–12 years old in this special education class. Many of these students have physical or behavioral characteristics that are identified with individuals with developmental disabilities; they fit the image of the "cast-offs" they are perceived to be in too many public schools. I like Emily immediately. She says she is "so excited" that I am visiting and that she can't wait to talk and get more ideas. I trust it. She clearly cares about her students. Her interactions with them are warm and genuine. Even as they go through some routines that seem patronizing and suited for young children, something about her style breathes life into this unusual class. She teaches with energy and enthusiasm, drawing students in, engaging them, facilitating, encouraging, expecting appropriate behaviors and participation from all. She celebrates their efforts and contributions.

Emily facilitates a full group opening session. At the end, she reviews the schedule written on the board and gives directions. Students disperse to individual "tasks / activities." Some are on computers; one is writing about a book she read. Others are doing various things with manipulatives, such as sorting coins, counting objects, or completing worksheets. Two students are working individually, each with their own adult (teaching assistants). There are planned activities (tracing letters in an alphabet stencil, putting large wooden beads on a cord, counting pictures, and tracing numbers on a worksheet). About every 10 minutes a timer sounds. When it does, the adult has the student check a picture schedule and move on to another (isolated, inauthentic) activity. One of the two students is Damien, the student Emily tells me she would most like my input on.

I am watching, taking it in, thinking about all of the students and staff, the routines, materials, activities, and possibilities. I try not to be obvious, but I steal frequent glances at Damien and his personal teaching assistant. He is sitting at a student desk. She sits beside him. Clearly the tasks are familiar. She is kind, but business-like in her delivery. There is a strip of tag board on his desk with three picture symbols for "work." Each is attached by Velcro. When Damien fusses or disengages, his teacher assistant points to these, saying, "Time for work, Damien..." When he finishes a short task (5–10 minutes) or the timer goes off, he removes one of the "work" picture symbols. When all three are removed, he "asks" for a break by requesting "crackers." The TA gives him a napkin with about one-fourth of a cup of crackers and sets the timer for one minute. After one minute, it's "time for more work, Damien." He complies each time and they move on to the next activity.

I notice after a little while that I am not the only observer. More than once, I notice that Damien is watching me, when he can glance away from his "work" to look my way. A couple of times I catch his eye. He does not look away when our eyes meet. I wonder what he is thinking. I am eager to talk to him and to try to get some things going. But I have only been here an hour. I hold back. I watch a bit longer. I take some notes. I walk around and check out what other students are doing.

About a half hour later it is Damien's turn on the computer. It is the only time since the full group lesson that he gets a little space. Damien puts on earphones and appears to be attending to the program his adult has opened. The adult is nearby, but not directing each step or leading the activity. It looks like he is doing a program practicing letters and sounds, like a kindergarten-level phonics program. I get my laptop from the teacher's office and open up an easy digital text that a graduate student made for a boy about his age. It has easy text, one sentence per page to accompany a photo; it is predictable and rhythmic. But it has realistic photos and shows the journey of a box shipped by UPS. I sit down at the computer next to him with my laptop but say nothing. I put the story in slideshow view and begin to look through it. I pay no attention to Damien. I am curious what he will do.

Within 10 seconds he is craning his neck, leaning into my space to see what is on my computer screen. I speak to him in the same tone I would use for my daughters, one of whom is his age.

"Oh, did you want to check this out, Damien?"

I reposition the laptop so he can see the screen.

"This is something a friend of mine wrote for a boy I know. His name is Aaron. He was really interested in delivery trucks."

He is looking at the screen. I begin to track the text with my finger and to read it aloud in a quiet voice. I can't watch to see if his eyes are tracking the print, but he is definitely paying attention. I hit the space bar to advance through the next few slides, pointing to each word as I read each page. The next time I finish a sentence, he is reaching. I point to the spacebar.

"Ok. Go ahead."

He is not aiming too carefully and hits keys. I take his hand and support his forearm.

"Try again."

He hits the space bar, and the screen moves to the next page. We go through the remainder of the text this way — me pointing and reading, he looking and (it seems) listening, and hitting the spacebar with some forearm support. There are about 20 pages in all. The timer beeps as I am considering another text to share. Time for Damien to move on. The teacher assistant walks him to his Velcro picture schedule. They remove the symbol for computer and look at the next one. It says break. He has a choice: music or something else. He points to the symbol for music. He goes to another computer near his desk and puts on headphones. The teaching assistant resets the timer.

I bring my laptop over to his desk, which is isolated from the rest of the tables and workstations. I want to try out some more activities with him. I ask his teacher if this is okay; she agrees.

He clearly enjoyed viewing this text on the computer. I wonder if I can get him to participate in some shared writing. While he is listening to music at another station, I prepare. I open another program on my laptop, a scaffolded early writing template. There are about ten "buttons" on the left of the screen, each with a small graphic for a sea animal (labeled): crab, seagull, whale, shark, fish, sea otter... Across the bottom of the page is a word bank of more buttons (A, The, is, has, skeleton, fish, mammal, crustacean...). You click on buttons from the bottom word bank and the sea animal buttons to construct sentences on the same page, entering whole words with a single click instead of typing letter by letter. Each word is read aloud as it appears. At the end of each sentence, each word is highlighted as the sentence is read aloud. I also grab a small whiteboard, a marker, and a tissue.

The timer beeps. Damien's break is over. The teaching assistant tells him to go to his desk. He wanders over, looks at me and my laptop, but does not sit down. I point to the chair.

"Hi Damien. Let's sit down." I tap the chair beside me. "Do you want to do some writing?" He looks at me, my laptop, and other materials on the desk, and stands, rocking. I point to the chair again. He settles in beside me.

"Let me show you this program. This one is about sea animals. We can do some writing about sea animals. Let's see what they have."

I point to the "buttons" on the left side of the screen and read each aloud: "Seagull, crab, fish, shark, sea otter, whale..."

He is definitely watching and paying attention.

"Watch how this works."

I use the mouse to click on word buttons at the bottom and one on the side to construct the sentence "A sea otter is a mammal." I say each word aloud as I click on it.

When I hit the period key, the computer reads the whole sentence.

"Do you want to write something?" I ask and write on the whiteboard: Yes / No.

He immediately points to yes.

I ask him, "What do you want to write about?"

I write three choices from the animals listed on the whiteboard, saying each aloud."You could write about a seagull, or a crab, or a whale. Do you want to write about one of those?" He points quickly — I think to crab. I check again.

"Sorry, Damien. I'm not sure about your answer — which one? Seagull, crab, or whale?"

He points again. Definitely crab. I erase the whiteboard. He grabs for the mouse. I slow him down, placing my hand on his and the mouse. "Let's think about what you want to write. You can use these words on the bottom."

I point to each and read the list to him: "A, the, is, has, crustacean, fish, mammal, skeleton shell." I do this at a normal pace – just fluently reading each while I point. I draft the beginning of a sentence on the whiteboard.

"Do you want to start something like this? The crab..."

I point to the button for the word THE on the bottom list. He uses the mouse and clicks on it. The word "The" appears above on the screen.

I read from the whiteboard, "The crab..." I point to the animal buttons on the left, but not specifically to crab.

Damien locates crab with the mouse and clicks on it. Actually, he holds the mouse button down, and it enters three times on the screen. His draft says, "The crab crab crab." I take the mouse and delete the extra ones. He does not resist. I point to the beginning of his sentence on the screen and read aloud, "The crab..."

"What do you want to say about the crab?" I pause for a moment, even though I know he can't tell me.

"How about 'has'? Would 'has' work here?"

I point below. He clicks on "has" and it appears next in his sentence. Again, I read, "The crab has..."

"What's next?"

He does not respond. I point to the word "a" in the bottom word bank and leave my finger there, saying "'a'? The crab has 'a'."

He clicks on "a."

"Ok what do you want to say Damien? The crab has a what? Let's see if there are any words here that would fit."

I re-read a few of the choices from the word bank, and write two on the whiteboard: shell, skeleton.

"Do you want one of these? Shell ... skeleton?"

He points to shell.

"Ok," I say, then point to shell in the word bank. He clicks on it with the mouse.

"Sounds like you are finished with this sentence. Can you put a period there?"

I point to the button in the bottom word bank for the period. When he clicks on the period, it is inserted at the end of his sentence and the computer reads the whole sentence aloud: *"The crab has a shell."*

I say, "That makes sense Damien. Crabs do have shells, don't they? It's a good sentence. Want to write about another animal?"

Damien signs something – not once, but three times as he rocks forward in his seat. I know very little sign language, but I know this sign. He is sure as he taps his fingertips together again and again.

"More. More. More."

"You want to write some more? Okay."

We go through the same steps. He chooses another animal (whale this time) and using the whiteboard and some pointing, together we figure out the words to construct another sentence. "A whale is a mammal." Before we choose mammal (*"What do you want to say about the whale, Damien?"*), I wonder if he knows this. I put the two choices on the whiteboard: fish and mammal.

I say, "A whale is a.... Do you know this, Damien? Is a whale a fish or a mammal?"

I say this conversationally – just wondering. It's not a test or anything.

He seems to be listening. He does not respond.

So I move on, nonchalantly, saying, "Whales are actually mammals. They live in the ocean with fish, but they breathe air like us – through the blowholes in the top of their heads."

I re-read his sentence from the screen. "A whale is a ...." I point to the word mammal in the word bank, and say, "Your turn."

He clicks on it and "mammal" appears in his sentence above.

"Go ahead and put a period at the end. Sentences need some punctuation."

I point. He clicks. The period is inserted, and the computer highlights each word and reads his sentence aloud: "A whale is a mammal."

He seems interested and pleased when the sentence is read aloud.

I continue with my conversational teacher talk. "So far you have a couple things here about sea animals." I re-read the two sentences to him as I point to the screen: "*A crab has a shell. A whale is a mammal.* Do you want to write some more?"

Again, he immediately signs, "More, more..."

This time as we are going through these steps, he lets go of the mouse and reaches for the keys at one point.

I say, "Oh you want to type your words. Okay. That's fine..."

I refer him back to the partial cloze sentence we have on the whiteboard. He is reaching for keys with his whole hand. He hits three or four at once. I delete these and say, "Can I help you?"

I take his hand and help isolate his index finger, saying, "Give me your pointer finger..."

His hand and fingers are loose — too loose. I gently hold his other fingers against his palm, supporting this position to keep his index finger out. I get him in the general area of the letter he needs to type next, but not finding the letter for him. I speak quietly as we go, naming each letter. "The T..."

He types the T.

I say, "H."

He seems to be looking for it on the keyboard. Again, I get him close. He doesn't seem to see it in the sea of letters. I point to it quickly with my free hand.

"Here it is, H."

He enters it right away. He glances at the whiteboard.

"Good — let's see what you need next." I point to the "e" on the whiteboard in "the." "T-h-*E*..."

I am still supporting his hand and arm. But I just help hold his hand up over the keyboard. He finds the E and types it without my help. We finish the sentence and the computer reads it aloud.

He does not need this program with the whole words. He keeps reaching for the keyboard. He wants to construct his own words. He evidently knows how this works — the letters on the keyboard make words. I underestimated him. This whole word software is too easy for him.

We have been working for maybe 15 minutes. Damien has been totally absorbed in it. He is wiggling around now. He sort of bangs his head on my shoulder. My impression from watching him through the morning is that he has sensory integration needs.

"Do you want a squeeze Damien?" I wrap my arms tightly around his shoulders, pulling him close to me, slowly give him a firm hug. He allows me to do this but is still moving around a lot.

"Do you need a break Damien?" I write on the whiteboard: *Yes / No.*

He points quickly to yes.

He grabs for the marker. I hand it over.

He writes on the whiteboard: *Crackers.*

"Sure. You can have some crackers and take a short break."

I look up. Peter and Emily (the teacher) have been watching intently from halfway across the room. His teaching assistant goes off to the "office / kitchen" and returns with a handful of goldfish crackers on a napkin. She sets the timer. Damien starts eating immediately. I stand up and take my laptop.

I realize that I have been totally unaware of the other adults. In my previous experience, I would often have been highly conscious of my audience under conditions like this, and anxious about my "performance." I might feel anxious about whether I could get the student to respond, worried about my credibility and what teachers would think if I could not. Today, I realize in this moment, was different. It was just me and Damien, present to each other in each moment. We were clicking, too. I could feel it. I know he could too. I don't give the adults another thought. The teacher-part of me quickly summarizes in my mind what Damien has shown me related to his literacy understandings and abilities.

- He likes to participate in writing – though a lot of the content came from the template and my suggestions. He was active in making choices for some key words and sustained his interest and engagement, even asking for "more."
- He knows some things about how to use a computer. He can use a standard mouse pretty well to navigate and select things. He knows his way around the keyboard to some extent; after a while I helped less and less, and he began to locate more than half of the letters he wanted on his own.
- He attends to a model and can copy letters and words; more than once, he was looking back and forth between the screen and the whiteboard as he was entering letters for a word.
- He can identify his preferences from up to at least three choices by pointing.
- He can write letters and some single words legibly and fluently, spelling some from memory (e.g., crackers).

- He needs some physical support to use a standard keyboard. His movements sometimes seem random; he does not seem able to isolate his index finger and keep it isolated. Providing some support to hold up his wrist and some gentle physical resistance seemed to help him select letters more accurately.

I am thinking about what else Damien and I might do after this short break. I search a bookshelf in the classroom for a text we might share. Mostly there are baby-ish fictional picture books. I finally find a nonfiction picture book on animals. I open it and skim through. A different animal is profiled every two pages. The pictures are realistic. The text is short, two paragraphs on one page and a box with a few more facts on the facing page. I skim a couple of entries. I want to share some reading and writing with Damien around some content. This book can work.

I go back to his desk. I have the book, the whiteboard and marker, and my laptop. The timer goes off. Damien sits down beside me. He signs, "More."

"You want to write some more. We will. Here's what we'll do."

I write on the whiteboard, speaking as I create the list.

"First, we're going to read." I write on the whiteboard:

1. Read a book.

"Then we are going to write." I write on the whiteboard:

2. Write.

He reaches for the laptop. I put it aside and point to the whiteboard.

"We will write some more Damien. I promise. But first we're going to read. Then we will write again."

I set my laptop on the floor. He seems okay about this, even though he clearly wanted to write.

I show him the book and talk to him about it, in a normal, mature conversational tone.

"Check this out. This book is about different wild animals. It has a lot of information and facts about them. We're going to read about one."

I open to the table of contents. I read through some of the animals listed. Then I open to the page on dolphins and write on the whiteboard as I say,

"Do you want to read about ... Dolphins?" (writing "Dolphins" on the whiteboard).

I open to a page about dolphins. "Or do you want to read about ... Sharks?" (adding "Sharks" to the whiteboard).

Damien points quickly to dolphins.

"Ok. Let's read about dolphins."

I erase the whiteboard and sketch out a graphic organizer, talking through it as I construct the parts of the web.

"Ok Damien, let's think first about what we are going to read about dolphins..."

I write "Dolphins" in the center.

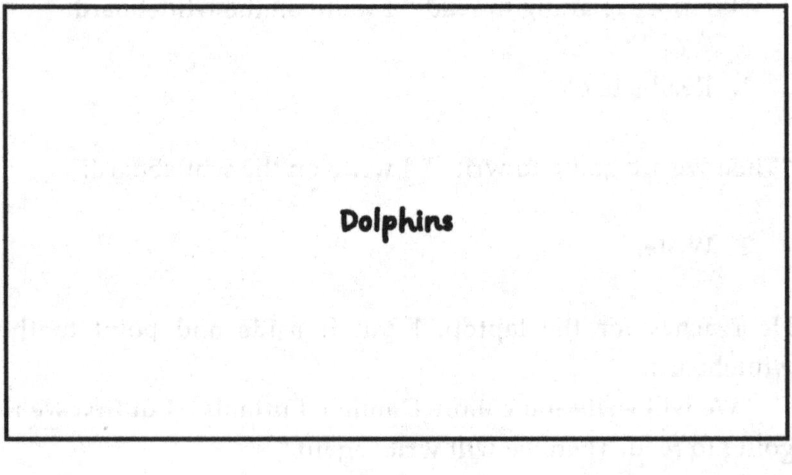

Then I go through the rest of the components, adding each to the web as I identify it. "We are going to read about dolphin life; kinds of dolphins; and how dolphins breathe." Referring to the completed graphic organizer, I say, "Okay, so as we read, let's think about these things and what the book tells us about each."

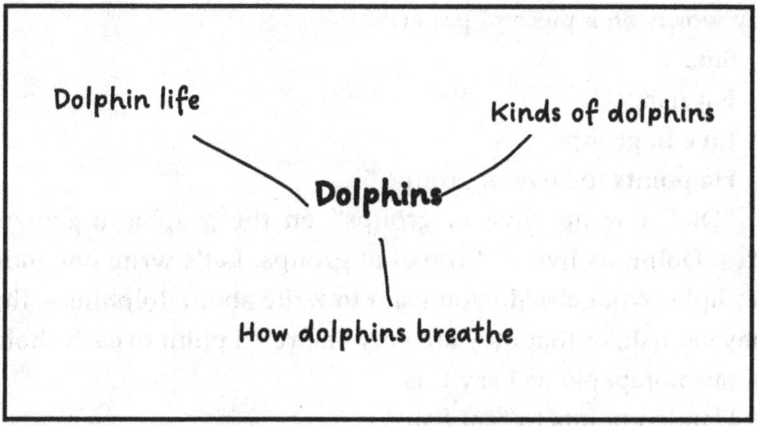

> "Dolphin life, how dolphins breathe, kinds of dolphins. Let's see what we learn."

I present the book and take his right hand again. "Can you give me a pointer finger again?" I ask. I help him isolate his index finger. I hold his hand and help him to track the print with his finger as I read aloud softly. At the end of the first paragraph, which is about dolphin life, I stop and present the whiteboard.

"Ok, Damien. What did the book tell us about dolphin life?" I ask, pointing to the part of the web about dolphin life. "Let's pick two facts to write down here on our board."

I restate four facts from the reading, summarizing, "We read that most dolphins live in the ocean, they live in groups, they are very smart, and they eat fish." I refer to the book as I say these. "Like here in these pictures. Look — it shows how they swim together in groups. And here are some dolphins chasing and eating fish. Here are more dolphins playing and doing tricks together."

Damien looks at the picture.

"What do you want to add to our web?" I read from the whiteboard, "How dolphins live."

Again, I present choices from what we read, while writing key words on a piece of paper:

Smart.

Eat fish.

Live in groups.

He points to "live in groups."

"Ok." I write "live in groups" on the graphic organizer. "Yes. Dolphins live and travel in groups. Let's write one more example. What else do you want to write about dolphins— that they eat fish, or that they are very smart?" I point to each choice on our notepaper as I say this.

Damien points to "eat fish."

"Ok." I write "eat fish" on the whiteboard in the part of the graphic organizer about dolphin life.

"Let's read some more." I refer to the graphic organizer one more time first, pointing to sections and saying,

"So we read about dolphin life. As we read some more, we're going to pay attention to what this book tells us about how dolphins breathe and different kinds of dolphins."

I present the book. I read another paragraph about how they breathe. Again, I support Damien's finger to track as I read to him at a normal fluent pace. We repeat the steps with the whiteboard. Through the process he chooses two more examples: dolphins breathe air and have blowholes in their heads. I add them to the graphic organizer. It's more work than the first time, but we get this down and he has participated in making the choices. But we are losing some momentum. I feel I am pushing him to stay engaged with this reading activity.

He is moving around more, leaning on me and making some noises. I suspect he needs some sensory input.

"Do you need a squeeze, buddy?" I give him some firm pressure – three times. It seems to help. I say, "Are you ready to write Damien?"

He signs, "More."

I pick up the laptop.

"More writing?"

He signs again, "More."

"Ok." I open a new file in PowerPoint presentation software. It takes a minute. He is patient now, focused on the computer.

I open a title slide. I type the word DOLPHINS in the title bar, and say to Damien, "So this is our title page. This piece is going to be about Dolphins."

Then I type "by" and take his hand to offer support. "Who's the author?"

No response.

"Whose piece is this? Who is doing the writing? We need to write the author's name here. Is it Damien or Ms. S.?"

He types in "Damien." While I support his hand and offer slight resistance, he quickly finds each letter in his name.

"Let's find a picture for our title page." I go into clip art. Again, he is patient through the steps – waiting and watching. There are only three choices of dolphin pictures in my clip art.

I say, "How about one of these?"

Damien points to one on the screen.

"Ok – you want that one." I show him how to select it with the mouse. He clicks on it. I resize it on our slide and re-read the words at a normal pace, pointing to each word: "Dolphins, by Damien."

I open a new slide. "Okay – what do you want to write about dolphins?" I refer to the graphic organizer, pointing. "Do you want to write about how they live in groups – or that they eat fish?"

He points to "eat fish."

"Ok — what do you want to say?"

I sketch out a sentence starter on the whiteboard. "You could start something like: 'Dolphins eat ...'. How does that sound?"

He reaches for the keyboard. I support his hand. He looks back and forth between the whiteboard and the screen as he selects letters to type. I say the word and each letter in his ear as he types, helping him locate letters if he hesitates for more than a few seconds. I don't want us to lose the flow.

"What will you say?"

He points to fish. He types it in (with some physical support and resistance), looking back and forth between the whiteboard and the keyboard.

"Can you add a period since that is the end of your sentence?"

I wonder if he knows where it is. No response. I quickly show him on the keyboard. Here it is. He types it. I read his sentence to him, pointing to each word, "Dolphins eat fish." Then I ask, "Shall we add a picture?"

I take us back into clip art and find some pictures of fish. "Do you want one of these?"

Damien points to one. I let go of the mouse. He selects it and clicks on it. We repeat the process, one more slide, one more sentence, one more picture: "Dolphins breathe air."

He's getting more physically active. While some might think he is losing interest, I wonder if he is distracted by what is going on with his body, related to sensory integration challenges. I offer and give some more quick "squeezes." It's more work; I have to provide more facilitation to get through the steps. He's about finished with this. He leans over and gently taps his head on my shoulder a couple times. I ask if he needs more squeezes — two or three? I give him two more firm hugs. He does not respond much this time, but I want to have some closure to the activity, if possible. I put the slide show in view mode and show him the slides, reading each to him. He is barely looking now, merely glancing and then gently bouncing his head on my shoulder. I sense he's had it for now.

"We're almost done here, Damien. You're doing great. We're just going to read what we have written, and we will be finished."

I finish reading the last slide to him.

"Thanks for reading and writing with me Damien. Good writing. Do you want to take a break?"

I write on the whiteboard: Yes / No.

He points with lightning quickness to Yes.

"Ok buddy. Sure, you can take a break."

His teaching assistant comes over to help him choose something. He gets up.

I take my laptop, and our book and whiteboard. I look at the clock. Between the initial trial writing and the book and writing activity, we have been doing shared literacy for over 45 minutes. We took only one 2-minute break for Damien after the first 10 or 15 minutes, before we started the book activity. I suspect that this long a stretch is unusual for Damien. I wonder how it felt to him in terms of the time. I am surprised by it — for me, the time just flew by. I feel good. But it's not the big wound-up excitement (activation) that I might have spun into after an exciting lesson. It feels more like satisfaction, a sense of contentment.

I am keenly aware of the connection that I experienced with this speechless, dark-eyed boy.

After school, I sit down with his teacher to process our day and to offer ideas about possibilities. Our first exchange is about Damien, of course.

Teacher: "I didn't know he could do that."

Me: "Neither did I."

While Damien's teacher and others who knew him at school seemed quite surprised at his participation and understandings of early literacy, in hindsight, I have misgivings. I may have actually underestimated his literacy and intellectual abilities. If I met with him a few years later, even without a decent communication system, I would use similar approaches but would attempt to share more sophisticated texts with more age-appropriate content. I was relying on the experience I had with early literacy learners that day and the available materials. Since that time, I have focused on strategies for comprehension, content reading, and the use of flexible digital texts with students who have developmental disabilities.

In the days and weeks to come, I replayed this session with Damien in my mind many times. It was different from most of my teaching and consultant experiences. I wondered what allowed me and Damien to achieve this during this improvised session. For the first few months after this consultation, literacy aspects of our session were in the forefront of my processing. I was eager to try to recreate this kind of shared reading and writing experience with other learners who have developmental disabilities. In the following chapter, I describe my attempt to do so with another young learner, months later.

Chapter 3

Misha: Humility and Insight

I would like to be able to report that my experience with Damien created total clarity and an immediate shift to grow my understandings about how I might maximize my professional offering. The truth is, I was not such a quick study. While I was deeply moved and genuinely curious, it took some time, and yet another young teacher, to help me to fully grasp Damien's lesson.

The next opportunity I had for some direct work with a school-age student came a few months after I had met Damien. This student was a third grader, Misha, who had favorite books, enjoyed being read to, and loved interacting with peers. She demonstrated a strong sense of agency and leadership, often initiating with classmates to suggest or join an activity during recess, or during "choice" time at centers. Misha, who has Down syndrome, attended a typical third-grade class.

From the moment I began planning, I completely lost my way with Misha. I realize now that I became strongly attached to recreating the Damien experience. I did a few things that made sense, from my existing consultant repertoire. I observed her at school and at home and listened to her family and her teachers. While her classroom teacher had created a rich literacy program, Misha was excluded from most of the third grade reading and writing activities in order to receive separate one-on-one instruction in literacy from her special education teacher in another location. Still, it was helpful to see the classroom routines, and to imagine how Misha could participate. The special educator seemed well prepared as a literacy educator. I observed her offer a skillful, meaningful lesson to a small group of students who had mild disabilities.

However, Misha's specialized literacy instruction consisted of a sequential, lockstep, computer-based reading curriculum designed for students with intellectual disabilities. There were no books or teacher instruction or interactions around texts. This observation helped me to consider what other kinds of specialized instruction and materials might benefit Misha, especially since her team included two knowledgeable literacy educators.

I also met with Misha individually to conduct some individual literacy explorations. I had asked her parents if I could videotape our session. They readily granted this permission. Looking back, I realize that before I even met Misha, I was attached to the "wonderful tape samples" our session would generate. I was already imagining sharing these with my colleagues and with our classes of graduate special education candidates. I planned possible shared reading and writing activities and brought my laptop to include digital texts and writing software. But unlike my time with Damien, my teaching was grasping after this imagined outcome. I was picturing the interesting, shared writing products that Misha would create. These, too, would be excellent samples to share with graduate students and teachers.

Needless to say, my time with Misha could not have been more different than my time with Damien. I had great difficulty engaging her and sustaining her participation. I felt my frustration rising. I became rigid and increasingly controlling as I tried to steer "our" experience toward my imagined outcome. Some moments deteriorated completely into a power struggle between me and this 8-year-old child. We found no flow, no connection. Neither teacher nor learner experienced much success that day.

When I got in my car for the drive home, I knew there would be no tape of this session that I would want to view, let alone share. Worse, I knew it *felt* completely wrong. This "feeling" did not come from professional experience or assessment frameworks of effective teaching. The "wrong" feeling was something I felt in my gut. This was all wrong, not only educationally, but on a human level. I would have to reflect on this experience, one that I was far less interested in replaying, to continue to explore both today's lessons and my experience with Damien.

I only watched a bit of the videotape. It was painful. But I stayed present to the disappointment and heavy feelings it generated. I really didn't need the tape to recognize what had happened. I was not present to myself. Therefore, I was not available to be present to Misha. I had gone into this session arrogantly, with an agenda, completely attached to recreating a "powerful" experience for myself and generating outcomes that would serve me. The brief excerpts of tape I watched confirmed what I knew. Our interactions had been completely task focused. Our interactions were not about her, but about the activity and the materials, and my desired outcomes. I was mostly unavailable, having reduced myself to a taskmaster. As we proceeded, she became increasingly invisible to me as a child, as a learner. I was disconnected from my own experience throughout our time, unable to notice, to let go, to respond to the child. I knew what was missing — I had been completely unmindful.

As painful and sobering as this was, it was a valuable and necessary perception for me. While Damien had opened me to unknown possibilities, Misha handed me a much-needed lesson in humility. Insight emerged. Our teaching, like our life, can only happen in the present moment. I needed to continue to cultivate my mindfulness practice in order to grow in the direction of offering the kinds of authentic teaching that I had briefly touched with Damien. I now accepted that I needed to understand everything about my experience with Damien, and saw how I could cultivate conditions to explore, without attachment to outcomes or the desire to recreate a particular experience. Each student, each session, each lesson would need to be allowed to unfold spontaneously in the present moment. If I wanted to pursue authentic teaching, I would have to leave my ego's agendas out of it and show up each time to begin the journey anew, with a willingness to accept, and learn from, whatever manifested.

After a while, I was able to revisit my Damien experience with fresh eyes. I recalled how I had felt so vulnerable on that trip, and particularly the morning before I visited Damien's school. My personal daily meditation practice had been in place for more than a year. That morning, due to my escalating anxiety, I spent more time than usual with mindfulness practices, including sitting and walking meditation and listening to a recording of a meditation teacher's talk. My practice had been more concentrated that day, as I wrestled with my limitations in light of my responsibilities. That is when I realized that the fundamental difference that day was my mindfulness.

I was present and connected to myself, and my experience, as each moment with Damien unfolded. Zen master, Thich Nhat Hanh (Plum Village, 2020) teaches us that mindfulness is always mindfulness of something. On that day, I was mindful of my teaching, in a more concentrated way than I had ever before experienced. The literacy routines and my interactions with Damien served as the anchor for my mindfulness. Just as I know how to breathe, I did know quite a bit about how to teach early literacy learners. As long as I remained mindful and present to my experience, the teaching required little effort. All of my professional knowledge and understandings about reading and writing, and about students with disabilities, were available to me. Things I knew just surfaced as they were needed. For example, I just "knew" to create a visual schedule to introduce the multi-step reading and writing activity, to support Damien's hand for typing, to create a graphic organizer and preview the text before reading.

As I reflected on the differences between my time with Misha and with Damien, and considered other experiences with mindfulness, more understandings emerged. One of the distinct features of my time with Damien was a sense of coordination and palpable connection. I realized how this was like my experiences with mindful partners in other shared contexts. I recalled sessions with my counselor who offered deep presence, the sense of connection I felt when in many yoga classes, and my experience of increasing relationship with strangers on silent meditation retreats, where everyone commits to practicing mindfulness all day long, across all activities (e.g., sitting, eating, walking, working). Eventually I also realized that my personal vulnerability on that particular day also contributed. Dr Brené Brown's research (Brown, 2012) demonstrates that vulnerability is the necessary foundation for human connection. The very vulnerability that fueled my anxiety due to physical challenges, and the unstructured nature of the consultation that stripped away my control and sense of "expertise," sent me into Damien's classroom with an open mind and a wide-open heart. There was no separation between Damien as student and me as consultant; we were one. In Thich Nhat Hanh's words, we were experiencing the reality of our "interbeing" (Nhat Hanh, 2017) — we had no separate selves.

I came to understand that this time with Damien was an authentic, mindful experiment for both teacher and student. I was open, vulnerable, and willing to take risks as the session unfolded. It seemed Damien was available in these ways as well, making this a truly *shared* exploration. This presence allowed me to experiment with myself as a teacher — staying open to taking risks and trying things — to go to my edge and trust my experience and instincts in the moment, without any attachment to outcomes. I was able to adjust and shift to modeling, teaching, and supporting — to partnering as a shared thinker to keep our shared literacy experience going forward — together. This sense of connection, grounded in vulnerability and mindfulness, seemed to free both of us to access and spontaneously share our experiences and knowledge.

I was now clear that *mindfulness* was the necessary foundation for all stages of my teaching and consultant work. I reflected on how to bring more consciousness and respond intentionally to this work, and to trust, rather than "lead" with my professional expertise (which could easily morph into my own separate agendas).

My time with Misha reminded me that my mindfulness was not fixed but was (like everything) continually changing. In every moment of every session, I was still just as capable of being an *unmindful* teacher as I was of being a mindful one. One of my mindfulness teachers remarked to me once, "That's why we call it 'practice'—we are never finished; we never get 'there'." Misha helped me to recognize barriers to my mindfulness; things I can easily become attached to (even for "positive" reasons), where I can get caught and lose my ability to be mindful. These include some of my common human limitations, such as the sometimes self-righteous nature of my advocacy, perhaps grounded in the "expert" self I was so attached to.

Lessons Learned

After additional months of processing my Damien experience and holding the disappointment as I reflected on my time with Misha, I began to recognize how several elements of my experience and professional knowledge had intersected to support both Damien's and my success as partners that day.

My processing of my experience with Damien revealed that my emotional state and my language, throughout our time together, were the keys to creating and maintaining this steady energy of mindful presence, for myself and for Damien. My personal pattern and response to anxiety is to move and speak faster, to do more, to direct and push. This increases my anxiety, which fills the space and is often transmitted (unintentionally) to those who share it. My focus was to keep myself present and calm by doing one thing at a time, and by consciously monitoring my mental, verbal, and physical pace. Between and during activities, I focused (lightly) on operating at what felt like a "half step" slower than the rate my body and brain wanted, especially in the beginning. I was intentional about using language that was clear and meaningful for the literacy activities, but also natural, supportive, and collaborative. When I am present, my tone (verbal and non-verbal) is much more authentic. When I am anxious and not present, I am likely to sound falsely enthusiastic or offer empty praise. There is a steadiness that emerges in my words and my tone that sounds like my trustworthy voice when I am with a familiar, trusted friend who knows me well.

As I re-read this, I think, "This sounds way too complicated! How can I possibly focus on all of this at the same time — the literacy frameworks and moment-to-moment decisions, the pace, the talk, our tone of voice and movements and body language?" I can't. The good news is this: I don't have to. The most interesting finding about my time with Damien is that I *was not* actively working or striving with any of these. When I am prepared (i.e., bring appropriate professional knowledge and experience), do "enough" preparation for the session, trust my professional knowledge, and *when I am also established in mindfulness*, this is how my mind, body, and speech can respond. At the beginning of the session, I bring a light awareness to these elements (e.g., my rate, my speech). Once we settle in, my entire focus is on staying connected to myself and monitoring my own emotional / mental state to remain mindful. I notice if I am beginning to rush things or steer too much. I notice if I am getting too focused on the task; perhaps trying to "make something happen" to get a particular outcome or prove something. I slow myself down, breathe, and focus on my broad literacy purposes, on my self, and on this student, with me, right now. This is really my only job – to monitor myself in order to maintain my own mindfulness. When I can do that, and I am engaged in something within my capacity (e.g., teaching reading) much of the rest often just flows. This process with Damien seemed to reflect the description by one of my Buddhist mentors, of how she describes her work: "I show up, pay attention, and try to respond skillfully" (Joanne Friday, 2019).

When I am grounded in mindfulness, I move and speak from a place of authenticity and trustworthiness. I notice what is important and relevant about the student's literacy behaviors, and amazingly, I very often just "know" how to respond in the moment – drawing upon my professional knowledge to enhance the literacy exploration.

Mindfulness reveals not only what is possible for this student but, perhaps more importantly, *what is possible for this teacher*. This was what was so powerful and striking about my experience that day. After observing our work for nearly an hour, his teacher remarked about Damien, "I didn't know he could do that." Those words rang true for me as well, about my participation. I left the session in awe of my teaching experience with him. I didn't know I could do that. More accurately, I didn't know I could *be* that teacher.

I came to understand that my presence and mindfulness invited and supported Damien's ability to join me in this unscripted, but deeply informed dance. While I was facilitator, we actively collaborated. Teaching and learning are inextricably connected, as are teachers and their students. We "inter-are."

Chapter 4

Keira: Another Chance

Though my time with Misha was humbling, the insights that emerged were invaluable. Within a few months, I received an invitation to meet with another student, Keira. I welcomed this opportunity to apply what I had learned from Damien and Misha.

Mindful Preparation

Understanding that mindfulness was the foundation, I began to explore ways I might cultivate conditions that support my presence, before and during these types of consultations. I continued my daily practices knowing that my capacity for mindfulness was something that grew steadily over time, not something I could call up or turn "on and off." I practiced weekly with a small group of other meditators, since this seemed to nurture and help me to sustain and deepen my individual practice.

My daily mindfulness practice is something that I follow year-round, whether at home or away, weekdays and weekends, whether working or not. Each morning I rise early and, after a cup of coffee, I go to a quiet space in my home that I have created for my practice. When I first began my practice, I sat for just 10 to 20 minutes of daily breath meditation. The impact was noticeable, even within the first 2 weeks. My practice has continued to expand and evolve. Now my daily practice can take from 30 to 45 minutes. Even when short, I have two or three different practices. Typically, it includes some of the following elements.

- Beginning my practice, I light a candle, chime my small bell, or read a page or two from a text from a mindfulness teacher. This seems to orient my body and mind and helps me to transition to my practice.
- Next, I might listen to a recorded chant or song, or to a short recording of a guided meditation while I connect to my body and my breathing. This helps me to begin to drop into my meditation, relaxing my body and quieting my mind.
- If I have more time, I continue with meditation (sometimes a longer guided one) or meditate quietly on my own; or I might do a different practice such as bringing to mind five or ten things I am grateful for in my life at this time, or connecting to an intention for my practice (e.g., for being mindful in some part of my teaching or with a particular person). I sometimes take a minute to think about a positive moment I shared with an ancestor or mentor. I try to remember where we were and what we were doing, maybe some phrases or words we may have shared. I let this memory allow that feeling of being seen and appreciated to wash over me and fill me before I conclude.
- At the end of every practice, I try to stop and notice how my body feels and breathe three times to notice and enjoy the settling. Then I ring the bell three times to finish. I try to continue the mindfulness and notice my steps as I move to my next location in the house, even if it is only a short distance.

On days when there is more time (e.g., weekends), I try to prepare my breakfast mindfully, conscious of each step as I measure and boil water, add and stir oatmeal. Before I eat, I sometimes read a reflection to bring my attention to all who have contributed to bringing this food to me, reminding me to eat it with gratitude and mindfulness. For at least the beginning of my meal, I do not read or speak during my breakfast. There is no television or radio or music playing. Neither my phone nor computer nor the newspaper are within my view. I try to eat silently and slowly, trying to fully taste each spoonful, noticing the texture and flavors, and chewing carefully. I look out the window at my backyard, noticing birds at the feeder, squirrels, and trees. As I eat, I swallow each spoonful completely and try to really notice when I take another, again trying to remain aware of the experiences as I chew, taste, and swallow each bite. I still try to implement these mindfulness practices — beginning my day with intentional stillness through sitting and walking meditation, and sometimes mindful cooking and mindful eating. This helps to set my internal state to a calm and steady place. Even if I am pulled off or get upset during the day, I tend to react less intensely, and to notice and recover more quickly.

I also practice yoga regularly, trying to attend classes at a center about three times a week. I continue to walk outside each day in almost all kinds of weather. I try to take walks in more natural parks when possible, sometimes weekly, sometimes less, depending on my schedule. I try to spend my free time with positive, settled people. I am increasingly aware of conditions and people that strengthen my internal solidity and devote conscious effort to reducing my intake of things that increase my anxiety or fear. I try to monitor what I consume, including conversations and media, and especially my thoughts. I get news mostly from print sources, and rarely watch television news programs or listen to the radio. I don't watch movies or television shows that depict suffering and violence, even if fictional, as I tend to take these energies in. I try very hard not to multi-task at home or at work. I spend some time alone each day, and some daily time, even if just a few minutes, doing nothing at all. I find that intentionally slowing my pace of my daily life contributes to my foundation of mindfulness. This means I cannot say yes to everything and everyone. I have to prioritize. These changes and patterns have evolved over time as I make decisions about how to organize and spend my time. This is some of my experience so far with devoting part of each day to practices that cultivate my mindfulness.

After my Misha experience, I was careful to continue my typical daily mindfulness practices during the weeks leading up to any consultation. I sometimes expanded the time I practiced in the morning or added another sit, even if only 10 minutes of quiet breathing. I was also intentional about creating space in my life and not "over-booking" myself and adding stress. I would make sure not to take on extra responsibilities during the week or two before a consulting session. This included professional responsibilities, but also social or other commitments — hosting or going out with friends or family, or other volunteer work or projects at home. When my children were living at home, there were some adjustments during these brief periods as I cultivated mindfulness and contained my energy and focus. Meals were prepared but became simpler; the house was probably not as clean, and I did not commit to supporting additional activities for my children's schedules that required more of me. I slowly learned to ask for and accept more help from my spouse and my children for routine activities during these periods of 2 or 3 weeks before and after an evaluation. I was still present and available to my family members but dialed back on activities to conserve my energy. I also try to eat well, to exercise, and to maintain my sleep schedule.

The day of a session, I would pursue additional mindfulness practices. I would listen to a recorded talk by a mindfulness teacher as I traveled to meet the student. Arriving early at my destination, I'd stay in the car, set the timer on my phone, and close my eyes for 5 or 10 minutes of breath meditation before I went in. I tried to walk into the school or other location mindfully, coordinating my breath and steps, noticing each step as my foot touched the pavement, noticing the temperature, the sky, and the sounds, trying to stay present in this moment as I transitioned.

Flexible, Open-ended Collaborations

I remained convinced of the importance of flexible, open-ended and authentic literacy activities in assessing students with developmental disabilities. When I met with Damien, our activities were not structured as "tests," and did not require him to function "independently." Had I limited our activities to reading and writing tasks that he had to do on his own to prove his competence (or to confirm his incompetence), or used narrowly prescribed assessment protocols, I believe I would have learned little about his literacy development and other capacities as a learner. The interactive, shared, and supported reading and writing activities created a nonthreatening context where Damien could engage more freely in literacy activities. He and I could each trust ourselves, and one another. We could both try things and take more risks, without fear of mistakes. As we went forward, I had no expectations for how he would respond, or if he could do something on his own. I trusted I would learn something as things unfolded. My job was to stay present, to trust my literacy and teaching experience, and to respond skillfully to whatever presented. If he demonstrated a skill or understanding, I noted that. If he could not, I helped. These moments became open-ended teaching experiments for me. I had the opportunity to try a prompt, or model, or support him, which offered insight to what kinds of instruction and supports would benefit him at this stage. There were no right or wrong or good or bad prompts or responses, for him or for me. It was all good information, if I was present to notice.

The semi-structured, open-ended nature of these activities required me to try to be present each moment. As I went forward with Damien, I was conscious of my internal experience even as I invited and prompted his participation, observed his attempts, and responded with teaching, support, or feedback. All of these were seamlessly coordinated. Now I understood that coordination sprang from the mindful foundation, as well as the flexible, open-ended process that was never focused on Damien demonstrating his competence or fulfilling any desired outcomes or "correct" responses. It was Misha who helped me understand how flexibility and nonattachment to outcomes are critical to create conditions for mindfulness. My potential to stay unattached to a plan was completely connected to my capacity to be mindful.

I became increasingly aware of the conditions that were necessary for me to pursue these types of meaningful educational explorations. I needed to have enough space in my schedule on the days prior to and following the session to become more grounded and present. I knew that my approach could quickly become disrupted if I was overloaded, and thus attempted to do this work from a disconnected, unmindful state. I also became aware of my changing capacity. There were times in my life where other professional and personal circumstances needed my attention and energy, which reduced my capacity to bring the concentration and mindfulness this work requires. When I received requests during such times, my ego was often tempted, but my mindful self more often declined, recognizing my own limitations for co-creating the necessary conditions.

Keira: An Intentional Experiment

Months after my time with Misha, I was contacted by parents of another student, requesting assistance with an independent evaluation. In this section, I will share how I was able to intentionally apply lessons from Damien and Misha to facilitate educational explorations with this student, Keira.

Keira was an enthusiastic, motivated learner who would strive to do all she could "on her own." The youngest in her family, she had many interests, including playing the piano, Girl Scouts, and singing in her church choir. Keira was 11 years old when we met. She has Down syndrome and was identified as having a moderate to severe intellectual disability. Keira's family contacted me because their school district had determined that, based on her recent triennial evaluation and her "low IQ score of 39," Keira would no longer have access to literacy or academic instruction when she transitioned to middle school. Although she had made good individual progress in an inclusive program throughout elementary years, the Committee on Special Education recommended that she transition to a self-contained special education "life skills" class the following school year.

Keira's parents visited the recommended "life skills" class, observed, and met with the teacher to discuss the program. They noted there were no books or computers in the classroom. They reported that this program did not include any academic instruction or any opportunities to read, write, view, or respond to texts. Instead, the new teacher told them that students would learn things like "cooking and sweeping." At age 11, Keira had ten years of formal public schooling remaining. Her parents expressed a strong desire for her teachers to take her learning seriously, especially to continue to help her grow in literacy and academics.

Mindful Literacy Explorations

Keira and I met on a warm summer day. Her home was a two-and-a-half-hour drive from mine. I got up early, completed my usual morning meditation, and selected a mindfulness talk to listen to for the last hour of my drive. I arrived present, grounded, and curious. I had my bag of materials and a frame of ideas for the kinds of literacy experiences I might attempt and explore. I had considered a frame of literacy activities but had no solid plan. I would experiment (intentionally) with various activities, materials, and supports, based on careful ongoing observation of Keira's participation. I also had permission from her parents to videotape our sessions. I planned to revisit the tape for more focused observation later, and to support my interpretations to create an accurate and comprehensive report.

As soon as I arrived, Keira was anxious to read for me. She immediately showed me a familiar "take home" pattern book and offered to read it aloud. This was an easy pattern text with one sentence per page, with only one word changing (e.g., "_____ come from eggs"). She appeared excited to read, was focused and confident, and read with fairly appropriate rate and phrasing, and some intonation. My impression was that she had read this text many times. After that, she willingly engaged with every assessment and task I offered.

Before and during my time with Keira, I was very mindful of the kind of tone and climate I wanted to establish. Most importantly, this should not feel like "testing."

I tried to use language that invited Keira to partner with me, and my tone was respectful and conversational, rather than directing. I sprinkled intermittent nonchalant but relevant comments throughout our interactions, especially around shared texts. For example, when previewing photos in a text, I might add a comment to Keira's response. For example, she identified animals in one picture as "Doggies." I added, "Yes, they look like they could be puppies." Similarly, I told a few facts about ostriches, which were pictured in the book. "They are big birds ... humongous. They can't fly." And then I added, "Aren't these great pictures?" This created natural shared interaction around the text. We were exploring and noticing things about the book together; it was not a quiz. This helped me to create a tone that was collaborative in our shared literacy activities.

Before inviting Keira to read an unfamiliar, leveled picture book, I ask her to preview it.

R(oberta): Let's take a break and read a book. (I present the book and read the title aloud.) *What Animals Need* – it's by Brenda Park. Do you want to look at the pictures together first? We can have a picture walk before we read?

K(eira): Before … yeah.

R: So there is a picture of … what?

K: Doggies.

R: (Chuckles) Yes, they look like they could be puppies, huh? How about these? Do you know what these are?

K: Uh … penguins?

R: (In a friendly, positive but not "corrective" tone) Actually these are <u>ostriches!</u>

K: Ostriches?!

R: Yes. Ostriches are very big birds – humongous. They can't fly. They just run. (I am building background knowledge.) Aren't these great photos?

K: Yes…

R: (next page and photo) I don't know what kind of bird that is. Do you have any idea?

K: Water.

R: Yes, it is drinking some water… (next page) And what is this?

K: Uh … polar bear?

R: Panda bear! (Again, tone suggests interest, without judgment; this is shared support, not a "correction.")

K: (looks up at me, looks interested)

R: Aren't they cute?

K: Yeah.

R: What are they doing?

K: Eating.

R: They are.

During our shared reading, I also observe, noting qualitative indicators of Keira's readerly understandings and behaviors beyond the "scorable" data.

Keira was reading aloud a narrative picture book about the seasons. I was listening and collecting running record data, but also interacting about the text occasionally.

> K: (reading) "Winter days are short and children play in the snow." (Pauses, looks up at me, and comments) I love the snow… How about you?
>
> R: I do love the snow.
>
> K: Me too. You like snowmen, angels?
>
> R: I do. I used to make snow angels. I still make snowmen sometimes with my kids.
>
> (I then point to next page to encourage her to keep reading, to keep the momentum going.)
>
> Keira seems satisfied with my response and continues reading without hesitation.

This interaction felt very appropriate and natural. Keira was leading here — offering a relevant comment in response to the text and inviting me to share my experience. She seemed very present as she shared her thinking and while she listened to my response. While the reading stopped momentarily, she responded immediately to my pointing cue after I answered and continued to read. My impression was not that she was stopping to avoid reading, but that she "gets" the social aspects of reading. She understands that readers think about and respond to texts, connect to their experience, and interact with one another to invite and share this kind of thinking. Though she was a very early reader, her view of reading seemed broad — this is much more than "school work" or "getting the words right." I wondered if she would have shared this if I had set a more formal "assessment" context without all of the natural interactions and commentary in previous activities. She had some limitations with verbal language and articulation; she processed questions slowly sometimes. But in these moments, when things were calm and natural, she revealed more about herself and her thinking.

My intention and goals for this assessment were broad: to be present, and to learn all I could about Keira as a literacy learner, including effective ways to support her engagement and learning. Therefore, I could be flexible in my protocol, making this a shared exploration. The line between assessment and teaching was often blurred, as I shifted into instructor mode when she struggled, to model, prompt, or support her to succeed, and to notice what was helpful, or not. I would, of course, note errors for my data (e.g., during a running record), but I might also stop and demonstrate or prompt a reading behavior or clarify an interpretation, as if we were in an instructional session. I was as curious about what kinds of teaching, prompts, and support were most helpful to Keira as I was about what she could do independently. I want to know what students know and can do, but mostly I want to know what kinds of teaching, tools, and supports will be most helpful. None of us have internal abilities that are separate from our experiences, resources, contexts, and the people with whom we share these. I was curious about what kinds of teaching and learning conditions might help her succeed. What she knew at that point was valuable as a starting point but helping her teachers develop individualized practices that maximize her learning was my real priority.

K: (Reading information text about the Food Chain, stops at the word "grasshopper.")

R: (I notice she makes no attempt. She does not seem to be searching the picture or even saying the beginning "g" sound. I cover all but "grass.") Try this.

K: (Immediately) Grass. "Grasshopper!"

R: Read that sentence again and see what you think.

K: (Reads the sentence accurately and smiles at me.)

R: You knew this part (frame "grass"). Sometimes we can look at parts of big words when we are stuck.

I was experimenting with instruction and support. Could she learn to solve bigger words by finding parts she knew? What kind of prompt and level of support might be appropriate at this stage? I decided to offer a high level of support in this moment; she was responsive. My hunch was that this kind of prompting and modeling of strategic reading behaviors while reading continuous text would be beneficial to help Keira become a more skillful reader. Her response to prompts and support when she "got it" suggested she could, with good instruction, learn skills to use what she knew (e.g., phonics, words) to become a more strategic and independent reader.

Throughout our activities, I was very intentional not to focus on outcomes, or anticipated performance. There was nothing to pass or fail. Every activity was structured to maximize participation and engagement. This supported my focus on observing and yielded information about both teacher and learner. We moved through activities steadily, purposefully, without rushing. I alternated the presentation of authentic activities (e.g., reading leveled texts for running records, viewing electronic texts, shared writing of a text on laptop) and skill activities (e.g., reading word lists, making words). If we stay present and out of "quizzing" mode, reading and writing continuous texts with flexible supports can naturally support meaningful interactions that need not feel like "tests." This was my thinking about alternating books and isolated "skill" assessments (e.g., reading word lists, spelling words).

I structured some of our activities as exploratory lessons (e.g., while reading continuous text, viewing electronic books, planning, and composing a writing piece). I intentionally experimented with various kinds of materials / tools, modeling, prompts and supports, noting what was helpful and effective for Keira. For example, I structured the writing component as I would for a writing lesson with an early writer. While this included shared and interactive writing, and a lot of support, I wanted to create a context in which Keira made "authorly" decisions and had an authentic, active role in planning and composing. The following excerpts from my notes highlight part of our pre-writing planning, as we co-created a chart to organize possible content. I scaffolded in several ways, based on my impressions of her abilities. I made some of the decisions; I chose to have her construct an information text, and I provided several "mentor" texts on different topics. These picture books were beyond her reading level, but reflected rich content and helpful format (e.g., graphics, layout with brief text descriptions). I created the structure for the chart, by proposing possible subtopics based on the topic she chose, and I scribed her ideas on the chart to keep the momentum going and to help keep us focused on content and planning decisions. From time to time, I re-read our notes on the chart aloud to summarize our organization and ideas so far. Keira was active in the planning and writing process, and took on an increasingly active role, once she understood the steps we did together (e.g., choose a fact for our story, add to whiteboard).

R: So, I was thinking you might like to do some writing on my laptop. (I present three different information texts, all picture books. Keira is totally focused on my discussion and looks at each book cover as I share.)

R: We could write a story about ... Elephants. (Text title *100 Facts*.) We could write a story about ... Mummies.

K: Oh—cool!

R: (Showing next book.) Or we could write a story about ... Weather. What do you want to write about? You pick.

K: Okay. (She considers all three books.) Ummm. (Looking again at each book cover, taking her time. Eventually points to the elephant book.)

R: Elephants?

K: (Smiling at me.) Yeah!

R: I love elephants. Do you know what I think are so cute? Baby elephants. (Handing over book and leaving table to get whiteboard.) Do you want to look through that book for a minute and get some ideas for your story?

K: Yeah.

(I open a new file in Kidspiration, a basic graphic organizer software, on my laptop. I create a center bubble for a graphic organizer and type ELEPHANTS. K's eyes are on the screen.)

R: So this story is going to be about elephants, and who is it by?

K: Keira.

R: (Putting laptop aside.) All right. Let's get some ideas down about elephants and I will write them on the whiteboard. What do you know about elephants? (K is looking at a page in the book.)

R: Do you want to write about what they look like first?

K: Yeah.

R: Okay. What do elephants look like?

K: Big ears. (Watches carefully as I scribe on the whiteboard in a chart.)

R: What else do they look like? They have big ears…

K: (Searching the picture in the book. Gesturing with her hands from corners of her mouth to her ears.) Big wide mouth.

R: Wide mouths?

K: Yeah – a wide mouth.

R: (Writes.) Okay, what else?

K: (No response.)

B: (Referring back to picture.) Do you want to talk about any of their special parts?

K: Nose.

R: What is their nose called?

K: Big … trunk.

R: Trunk. How could you describe their trunk? What kind of trunks do they have? Long / short? Big / small?

K: (Searches pictures in book again.) Long.

R: (Flipping pages ahead slowly.) Let's find some other things about elephants.

K: (Stops me on one page and points excitedly.) I know! (Pointing to a page with a world map.)[Author's Note: I was surprised by Keira's excitement about the page with the maps. I recalled that her mother reported that she loved fourth and fifth grade social studies and learning about maps and other places.]

R: Oh, do you want to write about where elephants live? This part is about where they live. (Inserts new column on chart on whiteboard.)

K: I know — New York.

R: Some elephants live in New York — if they live in a…. What?

K: (No response.)

R: In a zoo.

K: In a zoo!

R: So elephants can live in a zoo…

R: (Pointing to map in book, continents are labeled.) Elephants live in these two places on earth in the wild. They can live in Asia, and (pointing to Africa) they can live in…

K: Africa!

R: Help me. How do you spell Asia?

K: (Looking at map.) Uh huh…. Asia is … A–S–L.

R: (pointing) That's an upper case I … and what's the last letter?

K: A! (Looking at label on map, re-reads quietly to self.) Asia...

R: (Points to map of Africa.) And what is this one?

K: Africa.

R: Can you spell Africa for me?

K: (referencing book) A–F–R–I–C–A.

R: Okay. (Reads list on chart aloud, summarizing.) So they look like this: They have big ears, they have wide mouths and long trunks; they are BIG animals. Where they live: They can live in a zoo. And they also live in Asia and Africa. (Flipping ahead in book.) I wonder if we can find out anything else, like maybe what they eat.

K: (Gestures to imitate a trunk with her arm and says) "Big trunks."

R: Yes, we have written trunks. Do you want to say something about what they eat first? (Stops on page about what they eat.)

[Comment: I wonder now, as I re-read this, if Keira was recalling that elephants use their trunks to eat. I perhaps redirected her too soon.]

K: Yeah.

R: What do you think elephants...

K: (Answers before I complete question.) Grass!

R: They eat grass. (Writes, refers back to book.) Let me read this sentence to you. Listen. (K focuses on text where I point and read.) "Elephants are herbivores, which means they eat plants."

K: Plants!

R: (Calmly raises question while writing "plants.") Do they eat animals? Or only plants?

K: (With confidence.) Only plants. (Spontaneously begins to read a section aloud.)

R: Show me where you are reading.

K: (Points.)

R: (Summarizes what K read.) Ohhh, so they can pull huge clumps of grass up with their trunks. Interesting. And look, it says they can also chew bark. What is bark on?

K: Trees.

R: What should we write?

K: (Reaches for marker.) Bark.

R: You want to write?

K: Yeah. (Writes a B and stops.)

R: (Spells next letters aloud.) ... A–R–K... (K writes, R re-reads list.) So these are great examples of what elephants eat. We have grass, plants, and bark.

After we completed and reviewed the graphic organizer on the whiteboard, we participated in shared / interactive writing to compose a short essay with facts about elephants, gleaned from this text. First, Keira copied headings to a web I created in Kidspiration software on the computer. (Keira stated confidently, "I can do this.")

Next, with my prompts and support, she referred to each section of the graphic organizer to choose a fact and construct a sentence about it (e.g., *Our heading says "What Elephants Eat." On our notes we have ... and .... What do you want to say about what elephants eat?*) I offered possible sentence starters and wrote each on the whiteboard. "You could start your sentence like 'Elephants eat...' or you could say ______. Do you want to start with one of those? Which one?" Keira would copy the starter she chose from the whiteboard, entering the words on the laptop. I would further prompt and support her to complete this as a meaningful sentence, first rehearsing orally:

"You typed, 'Elephants eat.' What do you want to say?"
"Grass."
"Say the whole sentence: 'Elephants...'."
"Elephants eat grass."

She would type, sounding out some letters and copying key words from the graphic organizer. Then she would re-read the sentence that she had typed. (R: "Is that what you want to say?") We repeated these steps for each topic, steadily composing each additional sentence.

This flexible format allowed me to tune in to some of Keira's individual characteristics more closely, in order to monitor my impressions. I would occasionally assess my interpretations (e.g., miscue or unique pronunciation?), and noticed that she sometimes knew more than her first responses to questions indicated.

In the following example, my tone remained calm and nonjudgmental as I supported her reading process to notice a mismatch and to use her understanding of the story to self-correct. My language tone was still one of partnership, but I also incorporated explicit "reading teacher" language and consciously prompted her to be in control of her reading process by having her decide if the correction now made sense.

K: (Reading.) The wind gets colder and <u>wish</u> comes.

R: Try this word again. (Pointing to winter. I wait – no response.) What season do you think this will be? (Wait – no response.) What season comes after fall?

K: Season…

R: Spring, summer, fall…

K: (Confidently, her face lights up.) Winter!

R: Does winter make sense here?

K: Yeah!

R: Go ahead read it again and let's see if that makes sense.

K: (Re-reading.) The wind gets colder and winter comes.

R: Does that make sense?

K: Yeah!

I used explicit instructional language to support Keira's reading: *Does winter make sense? Read it again and let's see if it makes sense.*

Even if she needs a high level of support, I send a message that I see her as a reader who is in charge of her reading, as a thinker. We were comfortable and connected, but we were engaged in very "real" reading instruction in this moment. My professional literacy teacher language reflected my presumption that she is a reader, and that I took her and her learning seriously.

Some of our interactions with texts suggested that Keira needed time to focus and process questions. Sometimes it appeared she was formulating a thought when I asked a question and shared her thought instead of responding to mine. She also frequently seemed to repeat a key word or last word first, but I sensed that these did not always represent her intended response. When I gave her more time or repeated the question, she could often offer a meaningful response. The following interaction provides an example of what I mean by this:

(Previewing picture in an information text, an easy picture book about wild animals.)
R: Look at this! This is a cheetah! What is he doing?
K: He has polka dots. Run.
R: He does have polka dots. Cheetahs do run. Is he running in this picture?
K: (Takes a moment to check picture closely.) Not so much.
R: What is he doing in that tree?
K: Sleep.

My hunch about this interaction is that Keira was already thinking about the animal's photo and noticing its spotted coat. The comment "run" may well be from her background knowledge about cheetahs. These relevant thoughts came out first, but it is possible she did not hear or process my initial question ("What is he doing?") while her own thoughts were sparking. I chose to affirm her comments, which were relevant, and ask again, rather than assuming she gave a "wrong" answer or was unable to understand my questions. I could let go of my expected response, and presume that perhaps she has thoughts, too, and these (and her language and learning characteristics) may make it difficult to hear and process my talk simultaneously. Under the criteria of a formal assessment, she would have just been "wrong"—and I would have learned less about her.

It seemed we were fine after this interaction. As demonstrated by what occurred immediately after this, she evidently did not feel quizzed or wrong.

R: (Turning back to front cover.) You want to read?
K: Sure!
R: Go for it.
K: Thanks so much! Okay. (Reads title in a confident "presentation voice.") "What animals need..."

Keira and I shared a number of literacy-related activities for nearly 2 hours before lunch, and for about 90 minutes after. Throughout the day, Keira was a highly engaged, enthusiastic, and persistent literacy partner. Our day had been filled with friendly, supportive interactions through shared texts we read and constructed. It seemed we both experienced connection and ease.

I spent the next week reviewing my notes and data, as well as videotapes, to make sense of what our time together revealed about Keira as a reader, writer, and learner. I developed a formal report summarizing her developmental reading and writing abilities and needs with detailed recommendations for access to quality reading and writing instruction and tools as a central part of her daily education program. By the end of the summer, I learned that the district had changed its recommendation for Keira's educational program based on this report. She would not go to the "life skills" class. She would have continued access to literacy instruction and modified academics.

But I felt the real success the day I left, before the report was even written or her program revised. I drove home with a deep sense of satisfaction. It was not about Keira's literacy engagement and performance, though she was able to demonstrate a great deal of helpful information. On that day I knew I had succeeded in maintaining my mindfulness for many moments of our time together. I had met my intention. There was connection and flow. I had invited without directing. I remembered to support lightly while I listened and observed what Keira was offering in many moments, available to see and hear her. We let things unfold with curiosity and skillful guidance, with no concern for outcomes.

In subsequent months and years, I had the opportunity to conduct additional individual literacy explorations with students who have a range of learning characteristics. All happened to be learners with significant developmental disabilities, labeled as having moderate to severe intellectual disabilities and challenging levels of autism. My practice continued to serve me well in encounters with each, from first grader to high-school-age learners. While their characteristics and literacy abilities varied greatly, my growing understandings and ability to join them in a dance of mindful, shared literacy-based explorations revealed much about them as learners. These shared sessions informed my detailed professional advocacy reports to support authentic learning opportunities in their formal schooling and supplemental learning.

These repeated opportunities for deep, focused experiments with mindful teaching watered seeds that challenged me to reflect on my teaching practice in other contexts. It was during this time that I also began to reassess my broader teaching role, as a graduate education professor, through the lens of mindful teaching. The chapters that follow invite you to explore that shift, and lessons that emerged from those efforts.

Part Two

Engaged Teaching: From Intention to Action

Part two (chapters five and six) reports and reflects on my experience bringing these new understandings about mindfulness into my work in teacher preparation over several years. It describes the dance between my changing inner experience and my actions, as I took the leap to make mindfulness central to all of my teaching life. These chapters offer a glimpse into early stages of intentional changes in planning and instruction, as I became more present and open in my teaching with adult learners, who were professional education candidates.

Chapter 5

Re-Imagining My University Teaching

In this chapter, I zoom out to reveal how my growing mindfulness demanded attention in multiple aspects of my teaching life. I was a college professor whose primary role was to prepare special educators. My college teaching and other roles with pre-service and in-service teachers continued to challenge me to pay attention to all aspects of my experience, and to look deeply into how these resonated with my emerging intentions. I had been teaching in this college role for over a decade and my instruction was highly regarded by many students and colleagues. Some of what I began to recognize during this time of private mindful exploration made me very uncomfortable and threatened some long-held perceptions about my teacher-self. The insights that arose demanded real changes in my teaching practice.

In this chapter I share some of my experiences during an early, very intentional time of experimentation with mindful teaching over two academic years. Some of the content is made up of excerpts and insights from my journals that I summarized and shared with a friend who was also experimenting with mindfulness in her personal and professional life.

These reflections reveal that for me, the beginnings of this shift and commitment to mindful teaching came with many uncomfortable emotions, including fear and anxiety. Changing my teaching approach required me to take many risks and to pay very close attention to my experience during this phase. I wrote privately about my experiences on a regular basis. These excerpts offer my awareness of my inner experience as I prepared for each new academic year, and monitored my feelings, efforts, and changes throughout each semester. I had become conscious that the time had come to honor my commitment to mindfulness in all of my teaching. I was not at all comfortable, but I felt I had no choice. It was a matter of personal integrity. I took the leap.

As I was drafting this chapter, I told my daughter about the content. Smiling, she suggested a chapter title: "Damn it: Now I have to change my teaching!" How that joke resonated with me, recalling how I trudged forward, dragging all of my ego's resistant beings and voices along for the ride.

Preparing for Change

The following is an excerpt from my journal.

August

My teaching work continues to challenge my assumptions. It has been building for months, more than a year really. Now that I can be with it, I am acknowledging the realities.

Teaching is central to my identity — my perceptions of my "self." It has been my life's work, first with children, and now with adults. I care deeply about this work, about doing it well. As I look deeply at my orientation, my language, and my practices, I realize I have operated mostly from anxiety and control to fulfill my perceptions of a role as a "good" teacher. My anxiety about the quality of teachers (and my family of origin experience with disability) over-emphasized my perception of my role as gatekeeper. I want my candidates to be well prepared, to be thoughtful decision makers who operate from principle, and to be leaders in whatever systems they participate in. I thought the ticket was to give them the right content — to be sure they knew all of the important stuff (that would be my stuff). This content focus supported my perception of my role as "trainer / teacher" — that I had important information to impart; that I could / should define and shape my candidates' professional growth and learning. The combination of my gatekeeper role with my expert teacher role meant that I focused a lot on evidence (evaluation) — ensuring that I had enough data to support that they "got" the content — and had the foundation to become the teachers "I" imagined. Fortunately (or sometimes I think, unfortunately), I don't trust that anymore.

The new (and legitimate) anxiety lies in the reality that I cannot continue to teach in the old way. It also requires that I teach in a new way — one that is unfamiliar, one that I cannot even picture — one that requires me to bring my authenticity (translation: vulnerability) into my classroom —that I leave the mask and armor at the door.

When I step back and think about it theoretically, it makes sense that my anxiety fed my students' anxiety. Brain research confirms this is not an optimal learning context. My excessive focus on gatekeeping, content, and assessment was, perhaps, a bit reductionist. This orientation, carefully orchestrated (micro-managed) by my expert teacher-self, really constricted the system. The chance of any momentum emerging in this tightly managed system was slim to none.

While it is helpful to have a frame to interpret this on a cognitive level, it does not relieve the unpleasant feelings. Yes, I understand that relief is not the goal. Mindfulness is about seeing things "the way they are." I get that I need to stay with and experience these emotions if I hope to gain any insight about how to teach from a place of mindfulness.

This experience is uncomfortable, even painful. I have spent more than 20 years constructing and internalizing my perception of myself as a "good" (okay, very good) teacher. I also do believe that there is an authentic part of my inner self that is connected to my teaching, though, in this moment, it seems fuzzy at best. Once again, my ego is challenged in a big way — this time by the notion that it is possible that I have not been such an excellent, exceptional, outstanding teacher.

In fact, maybe I have had it ***all*** *wrong.*

While I hoped to inspire and empower my candidates, it seems likely that my practice has done the opposite — encouraging focus outside of themselves and discouraging them from finding and trusting themselves.

Intentional Practice: Beginnings

Fall

This reflection summarized my first semester-long experiment implementing changes to my college teaching with a focus on mindfulness.

I had been formally exploring and practicing mindfulness for more than a year. My summer had been full of momentum as the pace and intensity of my self-work seemed to proceed at breakneck speed. I planned and experimented with four changes in my teaching last fall that flowed from my mindfulness based personal work.

- *No more performances. While I was in therapy and experiencing and allowing much more vulnerability (something I had neatly avoided acknowledging for decades), I seemed to "lose" my ability to "teach." I suddenly had no spark, no passion, no rhythm. I was boring. I felt lost. It became clear before I began the fall semester that my false self "needed" to play off of an audience. I had a style for workshops and teaching that sent out what I thought was enthusiasm and energy (read: anxiety) and my students / participants got "stirred," engaged (read "anxious") and we got that "energy" flowing – moving back and forth (trading anxiety and self?). People seemed to like this style. Sometimes it was like stand-up comedy. I became quite attached to the feeling and the praise that it often prompted.*

When I began to allow vulnerability into more aspects of my life, I could no longer find this "passion" or bring this "energy" to my teaching. Well, I could sometimes, but I could no longer count on being able to access it. Once I understood this, I made a conscious commitment to monitor and avoid this behavior. I would tolerate what, at times, felt boring. I would try to teach without depending on my students to "feed" my false self, or to make me "feel good." That is, I would not give up self in this way in my teaching. I would let go of this aspect of inauthentic "other-focus" that required continual affirming feedback from my students during teaching. This went pretty well. I was calmer. While there was still a strong content focus, we had more authentic interaction, I did not "perform." I did not give in to playing this role.

- *Let go of over-planning. I worked on finding what a reasonable and helpful level of class preparation meant for me and my students. I intentionally departed from the lengthy, detailed over-planning that I had always depended upon.*
- *Reduce the number of assignments. I cut the number of graded projects / papers literally in half. I realized that I did not need this much information to assess a candidate's learning. This requirement for excessive evidence was an example of my anxiety-based gatekeeping energy.*
- *Reduce and revise assessments focusing on essential competencies. I always experienced a great deal of anxiety around people who were not meeting objectives, some of whom failed. As individuals who were at risk of not succeeding emerged, I recognized how I would distance from them and obsess (mentally) about their poor performance. I would drive myself crazy, alternately blaming them and questioning myself about my perceptions (in my head or to others). I took it very personally when people did not do well. This semester I worked to get clearer on my perspective of "fair assessment" and to trust myself. I worked on not taking so much responsibility for their lack of success. A couple of candidates once again failed the block. While it was challenging, I was able to stay connected to each of them throughout the semester, felt clear and fair about my decisions, and was calm before and after the final assessment period.*

Spring

During this time, I engaged in reflective writing to look deeply into experiences from a three-part consulting experience from the prior year, which included my Damien encounter. I reflect on my inner experience and interpret how mindfulness supported and informed my work and understandings.

Consultation

I don't consult much. For two years I did no outside work beyond my regular job. Then last summer I agreed to follow up with some work that I had done with teachers two years prior. It was going to be something entirely different. I would visit sample classrooms that had been affiliated with a multi-year professional development effort. I would go to a new school and new classroom each day. I would visit, observe, and consult on the spot with the teacher / team of the day. I would debrief with administrators each day and then with high level administrators for each region. I would write a report for each region.

One thing that was great about this was: there was no prep.

One thing that was scary about this was: there was no prep.

It involved significant travel — three week-long trips. Two were far away. I don't like to travel and be away from my family (my kids are still school age). But I said yes because it was summer when they called. I was excited about the work, it related to my vision, and probably my ego liked it that they seemed to think that no one else could do it.

Then six months later, I had to actually show up and do it.

I knew I had to be very different. I knew that it was a good opportunity for my practice. I would have to be very mindful; I would have to touch my vulnerability. I would have to manage my false self and monitor constantly to avoid becoming the bossy expert consultant.

I was more than a little nervous. This was just loaded with conditions that prompted my unmindful old self.

Once I was out in the schools, I started to figure out how to operate. I was very careful to practice mindfulness each morning; that helped me to ground and to begin the day from a place that was calm and present. In classrooms, I would hang out and observe for a while, listen to anything the teacher wanted to tell me, and then start to try things out one-on-one or with a few students. Usually there were some kids they really wanted help with, the hard ones. An interesting thing happened. I was so intent on maintaining my focus on myself and my behaviors so I wouldn't mess up with the adults, I was totally available and present when I started experimenting with kids. So, of course, they often readily engaged with me and joined in. It often went really well, and adults were watching but they were not my focus because I wasn't performing this time. I was teaching from a different place. It felt good, trustworthy — but I didn't get all wound up over it. So later, when I was meeting with the adults, I did not present my list of priorities for changes. I would say, "How do you want to use this time?" And almost always they identified some of the same priorities I would have picked based on my observations. And we'd just have a conversation or sketch out some possibilities. I would know what to say and how much to share. I found myself using new language, like, "You could experiment with this or that..." I was not all that invested in whether they did it, or did it according to my suggestions when I left. Of course, we both knew I would never see them again. A couple of teachers were hard to engage — so I offered a little bit, and we let it go. One teacher was incredibly anxious and other-focused. After some time, she identified one thing that she was already doing pretty well that she said she wanted to think together about. So that was all we did. Most of the teachers seemed engaged and energized about possibilities during and after our meetings. Except for one who emailed me; I don't know if they really tried anything we talked about. And I was okay not knowing.

There were many good moments in and beyond the official professional work on these consulting trips. I won't bore you with the other details, like my first experience with a significant panic attack, anxiety-induced nausea and headaches, and sleeplessness. Nothing like a little extra vulnerability to get me and keep me in the right place to increase my presence and authenticity. These three trips required a lot of work and discipline. I was very conscious of what I needed to do to be responsible and to self-monitor so I could stay present and not get bossy and judgmental from anxiety. Though my body felt awful much of the time, it went well. I was satisfied with my ability to practice in new, unpredictable contexts. But they were focused, short-term relationships. They were almost all brief, one-on-one experiments, with children and with adults.

I was very conscious of the power of experiences I had on these trips. At first, I thought it was about literacy and students with disabilities (my favorite content topics). It took months to unpack it all and to understand that it was about me, about my changes, about my mindfulness and how it impacted my teaching. This experience really increased the tug to focus on bigger changes in my regular teaching context at the college.

The Experiment Continues: More Mindful Teaching

Fall

This reflection shares how I extended my mindful teaching experiments from the previous academic year and consulting trips to go even deeper as I prepared for another new fall semester.

I attempted to begin planning official course documents several times. I got nowhere and spent about five days sort of ruminating about possibilities in my head, off and on, for many of my waking hours. The anxiety was still high and getting higher. One day, I made myself write some things. It took hours to come up with three pages of notes and some very small revisions on my syllabus. I shared these with a friend, thinking aloud about what I thought was legitimate and important in the course. I felt encouraged and more confident that I could proceed. Then I did some reading that I thought would be helpful. It made me feel very inadequate. It put me totally over the edge with vulnerability.

It seems it was helpful, but not in the way I imagined.

The next day I sat down (filled with a sense of heaviness, which was probably about yielding), focused and worked calmly on course stuff for the entire day. I finished my syllabus and assignments packet.

While there were no major changes in topics or schedule, I worked hard on finding the right words and format. I cut extraneous description, guiding questions, and list upon list of assessment criteria. I focused more on getting the words right. Our words do reflect and shape our thinking and beliefs. Our words impact others. I softened the tone, moving the focus from all of "my requirements" to my vision. I knew when I was finished and felt satisfied.

Here's a sample excerpt of revisions from teaching documents I shared with students.

OLD:
Tutoring is an opportunity for you to develop and demonstrate an understanding of <u>teacher planning and decision-making processes</u> for individualized literacy instruction. As you get to know <u>your</u> student, you should be able to make planning decisions that are directly related to his / her changing abilities and needs. That is, you will demonstrate your ability to plan and provide "expert, intensive reading instruction."

Lesson plans and reflections will be assessed both individually, and as a whole. Your overall set of lesson plans should reflect a logical progression that clearly relates to your student's changing abilities and needs — as informed by your ongoing assessment (noted in summary notes and reflections). Your careful observation / analysis during and after each session (i.e., self-assessing your planning and teaching, as well as your student's participation and performance) guides your teaching and planning.

(Oh my! "You WILL ... You SHOULD ... ASSESSMENTS ... EXPERT...")

NEW:
Tutoring is a focused opportunity to engage deeply with your teaching. You will have only one student for this field experience, maximizing the chance to focus on yourself and your practice — to locate and strengthen your sense of what it feels like

when you are really present and operating as yourself while teaching. Rather than "plugging in" to curriculum materials and acting out "others'" prescribed steps, scripts, or roles, you can explore your growing understandings of teaching and learning as you experiment with your student within a frame of effective practices for literacy learning. Most important will be your attention to your teaching and assumptions as you notice patterns and make adjustments. Pay close attention each lesson to your presence and connection, your language and behaviors, and how your student responds.

For example, when your student gets stuck during reading, do you get anxious? Do you share your anxiety through changes in your body language, or through your tone or words? Do you jump in right away to help or tell the student what to do? Does your behavior seem to be followed by the student "freezing up" or looking to you to rescue him or her? How might you experiment with your behavior in these moments? How might you self-monitor and not respond automatically from your anxiety in future lessons? Notice what happens (for you and the student) when you try a different behavior.

Of course, I am talking to myself as much as to them about teaching as I write the new lines.

I understand that the words on the page that I have labored over are not the changes. The real changes can only happen live, in the classroom, in the moment. As much as I would like to be able to "do" some of that hard stuff up front, to get on top of it — to "get those new things in place" ahead of time — it is not possible.

While I have taught this class before, I have never taught "this" class before. We will come together as a new community, with brand new connections to the many other systems we each function in. Things will change in our system week to week — because of our individual changes, changes in our evolving new system and changes in other systems in which we function.

My preparation will be important. My focus needs to be more about preparing ***myself*** *than preparing my content or materials. Every single class, I need to start from presence, to pay attention, move toward the center, to manage the anxiety, to monitor the inauthentic expert, to allow the vulnerability... I have to try to sustain it moment to moment. That's all. (Yikes!)*

I knew that two weeks ago. I could not acknowledge it. It was so scary that I preferred to think about the syllabus — to find something concrete to work with.

So, why all the fuss about this preparation stage? Maybe it's this:

I trust the momentum that is requiring / compelling me to commit to some bigger changes in my teaching. It was important to me personally that the course documents also change in some ways to represent what feels like a significant shift. It doesn't matter that my new students won't notice or know the difference about the documents. I know.

I think that sharing my anxiety and plans with select others who are cultivating their mindfulness is also part of my process. It was going public — sharing my vulnerability. This is one way to be authentic. It was like making the commitment to the consultation last summer even though (precisely because) I knew it would require me to step up my efforts and test my practice in brand new contexts. Now that I have made the commitment official, I have to actually do it. I have to sustain it in my teaching context for 3-plus hours per class, several times a week. I have to translate the new behaviors from one-on-one interactions to the group of 20 of us. Unlike my consultation visits, I will see my students again and again.

Now I am anxious.

At least the syllabus is finished.

Deep Practice: Mindful Student Conferences

Staying connected and engaging mindfully with any individual graduate students who were struggling remained a key focus for my mindfulness experiments this second year. All of my adult learners were master's candidates who are certified, but inexperienced and unemployed elementary teachers. Most have just completed their undergraduate program in elementary education and moved right into a graduate program in special education to earn a second certification as special educators. At that time, regional opportunities for elementary teacher positions were extremely limited. Their chances for employment were exponentially better as special educators, due to shortages in this field. There were years when nearly any individual who held certification in special education could quickly find a teaching job. And the special education positions that were most available were those for the most vulnerable students, the ones with the most complex disabilities. My personal vision, and that of our graduate program, was to ensure that all of our graduates would be well prepared to maximize the learning of a wide range of students with disabilities, particularly in key learning needs such as literacy and developing successful behaviors. We also emphasized teaching and advocacy skills for learners who had the most challenging disabilities, including those with autism or other developmental disabilities. In our state, there is special education certification for many categories, including students who are described as having mild, moderate, and severe disabilities.

In any given semester, there might be one or two students whose planning, decision making and teaching performance was not moving toward the required level of competence in literacy planning and instruction for the special educator role. My anxiety would present and increase as I read their weekly lesson plans, which did not heed or reflect my ongoing feedback. Observing their teaching during tutoring and viewing taped lessons added to my personal stress. I hated it when my students did not succeed. I took it personally, attached to a perception that if I was a good teacher, everyone would have a successful outcome and pass. I carried additional anxiety because of my advocacy work with individual students and families. Frequently, I discovered that a student who was deemed too disabled or inappropriate for a meaningful learning environment was served by a special educator who lacked adequate preparation, professional knowledge, and skills. I felt a strong personal responsibility not to add to the pool of under-prepared, ineffective special educators who blamed students for their difficulties. I also hated the pressure and reactivity I experienced when I had to communicate with a candidate that they would not be passing. One reason for this was that it seemed hardly any faculty in my department seemed to give failing grades, especially to graduate students. A student who did not pass often engaged in an appeal process, which blamed me for "failing them." Parents (yes, parents of adult graduate learners) would sometimes become part of this appeal, challenging my decisions and fairness. Appeals would go from my department chair to the graduate dean, and sometimes to the president's office. I always had ample evidence of my extra support and feedback and clear data about student performance related to objectives, and my grades were never overruled. Still, this was an unpleasant process that could go on for weeks beyond the semester.

One of the program requirements was a six-credit clinic experience related to specialized reading instruction. The focus was on understanding the reading process, using individualized assessments, and planning and providing intensive, individualized data-based reading instruction matched to specific reading process needs. We met twice a week for the course. Each candidate was assigned a first or second grader who was having reading difficulties, and twice a week after school they'd engage in one-on-one tutoring for an hour. This was a big shift for candidates whose teaching now had to match their individual learner's changing needs through structured, multifaceted lessons that flowed from their ongoing data collection. In addition to my informal observations during every tutoring session, candidates also taped themselves for self-evaluation, and were required to submit two tapes they chose of full hour lessons both early and later in the semester, with written analysis. These were significant data sources for my evaluation and grading. I would meet with every candidate for individual feedback and coaching about the first tape. I also wrote extensive feedback on weekly lesson plans, which added new components through the semester.

When a candidate was not doing well in growing this professional competency, I suffered significantly. Stories would come up. For example, if a candidate consistently posted underdeveloped lesson plans or did not make changes related to my feedback, I might begin to have thoughts that *"She doesn't care about her student's learning"* or *"She is not putting effort into this course and field experience."* I realized my discomfort made me want to distance myself from this candidate. I needed to work with myself every week to keep showing up for them as individuals. It was unpleasant and difficult. I took lack of progress personally. I needed to stay present to both my intentions and to candidates' learning needs when communicating about their progress.

The second half of one semester I had growing concerns about Anna, and one other student. I held individual conferences about their second tape submissions and offered more intensive coaching. I encouraged them to submit a tape again in a week or two that demonstrated their response to the feedback.

Anna's additional tape showed little growth. There were only a couple of weeks remaining in the semester. There were not enough tutoring sessions left to demonstrate that she was solid enough in her understandings and teaching in this area to pass. I scheduled another individual conference with her to discuss her teaching.

That afternoon, I practiced mindfulness to get myself grounded and to clarify how I wanted to be in this conference.

Anna seemed like a nervous individual, and I expected her anxiety about our meeting would be high. Though I knew she would not pass, I decided to try to engage her with co-assessing her performance. I hoped this could be a kind and supportive conversation to help her engage realistically with her teaching, regardless of the course evaluation outcome. I would also be clear with her about where she currently was in terms of course requirements, so she would be aware that she was not going to pass this semester. But mostly, my experiment was to be calm, kind, and to remain connected on a human level as her teacher. It would be a challenge. I would try to show up, pay attention moment to moment, and try to facilitate our conversation skillfully. I knew I would have to self-monitor for presence and manage my anxiety. I needed to keep my focus on me and my internal experience.

After it had occurred, I went home and wrote it all down to document my experience in this situation with mindful teaching. I offer excerpts from my journal about our conference in the pages that follow.

Anna Conference 2

The following is an excerpt from my journal which I wrote the day after this meeting, reconstructing everything I remembered of our conversation.

This evening I had a conference with a student who will not pass the literacy course and field experience. Her final lesson tape was painful to watch. She seems so disconnected and tense and task focused. She does not crack one smile. The little boy, who is a very animated kid, is suffering in no time. He scrunches his face and looks like he is going to cry.

I think this conference went well. I was clear on wanting to support the tutor in thinking about her teaching. I kept it very broad. I first asked her what is going well. What are her favorite parts of the tutoring? What feels good?

Anna offered very rote responses that did not align with her tape or my observations. I probed a little. She stuck with her story, as written in her reflections, saying: The book was a good match. Anna continued, reporting that she felt she was so smooth and fluent in her teaching during the guided reading. "It felt great!" She added that she is more confident and clear in her teaching in this lesson. I just listened calmly.

I asked about the student. What are her impressions of what she enjoys most about their sessions? Becoming a little more realistic, she mentioned something about him getting frustrated. We explored that. How do you know when he is frustrated? Oh? What do you notice about how he changes or looks? Her comments were very accurate. She mentioned changes in his facial expressions and body language. I said, "Yes, I noticed that in the tape. Good for you. You are really noticing what goes on for him. I saw exactly what you are describing. I think it is really important that you are able to notice when things are not working for Ben. When does that tend to happen? Do you notice any patterns?" Anna responded that there are no patterns; this happens randomly and unpredictably.

She mentioned something about his short attention span. It sounded kind of like blaming his attention difficulties, like an excuse or reason for his changing participation. Though this "blaming the student" is a hot button for me, I remained calm. I went with this without judgment. Oh — is that a challenge? Yes. What are the challenging parts for you? She said she gets frustrated when he doesn't get it.

R: Can you give me an example?
A: Like when we talk about this all the time — read more slowly, focus, pay attention. And he rushes through the page and makes a lot of mistakes.
R: How does that feel for you?
A: Frustrating. We work on it all the time.
R: Yeah, I'll bet. And then?
A: I have to keep saying, "Let's go back and read it again."

R: How does that feel?

A: Frustrating.

R: How does Ben respond?

A: He doesn't like it. He does this. (She models, covers her face, scrunches her face up.) He shuts down.

R: How do you feel then?

A: It's hard.

R: It's really good that you notice yourself getting frustrated in those moments. What's that like for you? What do you look like and sound like when you feel that way?

A: I get serious. My voice changes. I'm like, "____" (She delivers a series of dry orders in a serious tone.)

R: Ah. How does Ben respond?

A: He shuts down. He stops paying attention. He does this. (She rubs her cheekbones and eyes with her fists.)

R: On a scale of 1 to 5, how would you rate this lesson in terms of Ben experiencing success?

A: (Pauses.) 2 or 3.

R: Why do you say that?

Anna goes on to describe her student's frustration behaviors and how they happened many times. It seems accurate based on my observations. I tell her so.

R: This is really good. You notice a lot. I think your observations are right on the money. If you were going to continue tutoring Ben (the program ends next week), how would you want to be with him? You know what it feels like when you get frustrated, and you notice your behaviors. You can't really get rid of the anxiety. It will be there sometimes. So how could you experiment with your behaviors and your voice when you notice yourself feeling that way – getting anxious? Feeling frustrated? Because you do notice that – that's the first step.

Anna is with me. She says, "Maybe we should take a short break, take a few breaths, get up, stretch, start over."

"Maybe — but I don't know if you need to stop the lesson to 'do' all that every time. What about your behaviors? You are clear on what you don't want to sound like. You know that your voice gets all serious and business-like. What do you want it to sound like? Could you imagine sounding different?"

She rehearses out loud: "I could say something like, 'Oh let's take a breath and try that again...'." Her talk is calm and fluent. She is smiling a little.

I smile back.

R: Wow. That really sounded different. It was not just your words that were different. What else?

A: I sounded different. I was calmer, friendly.

R: Yes. Your whole tone was different. And you were very fluent. It just flowed. So what is one thing you could experiment with when you feel that anxiety and frustration and start tensing up?

A: Change my voice?

R: Yes. Just take a moment if you need to and rehearse in your head what you want to sound like, and give it a try. Lighten up. Relax. Is there anything else you could try? Maybe about your appearance?

A: I could smile.

R: You could.

Anna smiles broadly.

R: That looks very different. How do you feel when you smile?

A: I feel better.

R: Yes, it's wild; even if we don't feel like it, just forcing a smile can help us begin to relax sometimes. How do you think Ben might respond if you do just those two things — or even one — smile and change your voice to a calm friendly tone?

A: I think he will relax.

I am also smiling now. I realize that Anna and are in this dance together. It is not unlike the Damien lesson for me. But Anna is suddenly animated. She has something else she must share. She is dynamic as her story spills out.

"I have to tell you about my day today. I subbed in a class with the worst kid in the school. Subs leave this class and say they will never come back. And I just joked with this kid when he started this morning and he was great!" She goes on to tell several stories about how she just got off on the right foot with this boy, Leo, and made an effort to make a positive human connection first thing. She reports that he was so happy and so grateful. He asked her to eat lunch with him and more.

"Anna, that is a great example. You get this piece about teaching from connection. You have had that experience. How can you bring that experience you had with Leo into your teaching everywhere — here with Ben, when you are subbing in other places? It sounds like you were present with him and relaxed. He felt that."

I then began to talk with her directly and calmly about how this self-assessment of this lesson felt much more real and trustworthy, admitting she felt frustrated and noticing how Ben was disconnected. I said that I didn't buy her early comments. It did not match what was in the tape. I said it was really good she noticed and could admit it. "This is not just about this course or a grade. My role is to help you develop your teacher-self. If you can't notice what is really happening with yourself, you can't develop your teaching. But you **do** *notice. Everything you brought up about yourself and Ben were things I would have mentioned."*

"Anna, this is being present and mindful. You know how it feels. You are not sure yet what to do about it, but you notice. And I think your observations of what is going on for Ben in those moments are also accurate. When I looked at the tape, I didn't think you were having much fun. Was he?"

"No."

"How do you know?"

She again gave examples of facial expressions, decreasing participation. We talked about a few other things. I offered more coaching on how her adjustments and support in the reading process have to continually support Ben's success. He needs to feel successful as she reads during these lessons (Ben is a very early reader). Anna identified some concrete things with prompts that she could try. But everything was connecting back to tone and presence and her success.

Then we talked about evaluation and grading. I went over the rubric, being fair in my scoring. She has still not met the mark in many areas for this graduate experience. My feedback was honest. I said, "I am not sure, but I have a hunch that if you can be more present when you teach reading, you will be better able to make decisions in the moment and make those adjustments. If you can take care of yourself when you start feeling frustrated, you will be able to do what you know." I then explicitly confirmed that she would not pass this course and field experience this semester.

She knew there were problems and did not challenge my assessment. She heard that she was going to fail. But she was calm and happy when she left. I did not destroy her. She was not doing much well. I felt pretty good about this one. She was not going to pass and was not even close. I had to turn her around. But she allowed it and really engaged with all of it.

This conference with Anna was a big challenge for me. But I was present and, like my time with Damien, I knew what to say and do as I facilitated this conversation gracefully, without steering or striving. In the end, there was bad news. She will get a failing grade. But I did not cause additional suffering. This is who I wanted to be as Anna's teacher, for the whole semester.

As I replay this conversation in my mind, I find it striking that Anna and I are working on very similar anxiety patterns about how we respond when our student is not demonstrating success. In past conversations with students who were not doing well, my voice and tone would often shift, reflecting anxiety and disconnection and sending a message of judgment. I know this place. My advice to Anna about breathing, working with her voice, and smiling is exactly what I became aware of in my own anxiety patterns and was working with in my teaching.

I would like to tell you that all of my challenging conversations with students who were struggling became easy and reflected similar successes. But each one is different. I know now that my job as a mindful teacher is to do my best to be fair and honest, and to offer my presence and connection as a teacher. Not all students could be as present as Anna: some were too upset that they were not succeeding, even with support. My goal was to be honest, and to do my best not to add to the suffering. Writing about my experience with Anna documented my progress in my practice and reminded me of what is possible for me when I am mindful.

Onward

I continued to build on these first years' intense experiments with my teaching and to trust the mindful teaching journey. Each semester I would try to be intentional in conditions where I knew I experienced the greatest challenges and choose some additional ways to stretch myself. After several years, I began some explicit sharing of practices with my students to support their mindful teaching exploration. I share some of these experiences in chapter seven.

It's not always easy to show up and be one's authentic self in the classroom or in other teaching moments – at least, it wasn't for me. I had internalized and constructed many stories about being a "good" teacher and having "high standards." My growing mindfulness practice supported my deep exploration of my assumptions about my teaching and created a real struggle that required me to be more present and bring authenticity into all of my work. What I learned from my close attention to my mindful teaching efforts those first years is this:

For me, staying connected to myself and my intention, growing awareness of my inner experience, and cultivating skillful responses are significant conditions of mindful teaching. In the next chapter I share my efforts to bring mindfulness to my responses to difficult situations, which, of course, continued to arise at times.

Chapter 6

Practicing with My Unskillfulness

As I reflected on my first two years of intentional experiments in my teaching, I recognized how mindfulness was transforming my offering in various ways. Mindfulness has supported my ability to manage habit energies so that I can more often be present and available to myself and my students in many changing conditions. It has supported my growing understandings of my professional content knowledge and effective pedagogical approaches for supporting teachers' professional development. When I am present, I am more open and vulnerable, but also able to access my capacities with little effort. I am able to experiment and learn from my authentic experience, rather than "role playing" to fit my assumptions or others' interpretations of good teaching practice. I trust myself. I have developed confidence, while remaining curious and open to new experiments about emerging teaching ideas. This has made my teaching rich and satisfying in ways beyond what I experienced in my prior professional life.

As I consider what is different about how I interpret my life, including my teaching life, one of the fundamental lessons of mindfulness has been the increasing ability to recognize and stay present with reality. One of my favorite teachings came to me very early in my practice in this Zen saying: "If you understand, things are just as they are. If you do not understand, things are just as they are."

Like many other humans, there are times when I don't like "the way things are." One of my habitual responses to these conditions is to make up stories, even if only in my own mind. In my teaching life this might take the form of judging or blaming a student who is not performing well, perhaps thinking they are not working hard or that they don't care enough about their professional development. Or, if I create suffering through my own behaviors or interactions, I might construct stories about the other person's performance or characteristics instead of owning my unskillfulness. I would like to report that mindfulness has eliminated these behaviors, including this thought pattern, but it is not always so. However, more often now, I can notice my thinking. I can let go of the part that is my story and just recognize conditions for what they are. For example:

- Sarah is struggling with her decision making to match individualized reading instruction to her student and data.
- Juan is not yet matching his instruction to his student's reading needs and may not pass this course and field experience.
- I was not present to listen when my colleague tried to explain her position.
- I was unskillful in that interaction with my student teacher.

The above statements are observations of "the way things are" without added stories that place blame or add judgments. When I can stay present to more accurate observations, even undesirable ones, I am able to stay connected and often respond skillfully.

The first step is always to recognize when I am caught in my stories (always about others). My stories emerge when "the way things are" is causing anxiety. With a growing foundation of mindfulness, I am more likely to recognize the stories popping up in my head that are focused on the other person and to understand that they are just my stories. This is one of my patterns of responding to "things being the way they are" that I perceive as unpleasant. Although stories still come up in my head, I am less likely to tell them to others, and I can let go of them sooner to explore and own my experience. Letting go of my stories is necessary to me to accept that *"things are just as they are"* — even when I do not yet understand why.

The next step is to acknowledge and be with my discomfort and take time to choose a skillful direction or response that relates to the actual conditions that are presenting. When I accept "the way things are," I must also accept that I will very likely continue to feel uncomfortable. Mindfulness includes being with my experience, whether it is pleasant or unpleasant. But adding my stories and replaying them (even in my head) actually makes things worse. It keeps spinning and increasing my anxiety, and it solves nothing. Things may be unpleasant, but I can choose not to make my experience even worse with my stories.

In this chapter I share some examples that illustrate how mindful teaching is not always a blissful experience, as well as some of my experiments with intentional responses. I will also offer how, in numerous situations, I have applied a practice from Zen master Thich Nhat Hanh called "Beginning Anew" (2009), to do my best to respond skillfully, especially when I have not lived up to my intention to be present and mindful in my professional role.

Preparing Teacher Decision Makers

In my work preparing special educators, my responsibilities included a graduate course and reading clinic (structured tutoring program) for young elementary students who needed supplemental instruction in reading. I loved this part of my work, and continually explored ways to support teachers' growing abilities to assess and understand a student's reading process and provide effective individualized instruction. Providing individualized reading instruction is a key competency for special educators. Many learners with disabilities struggle with reading, but can become effective readers with good, specialized instruction. This is fundamental to their success in school and beyond. One of the greatest challenges for my candidates, who are all certified elementary teachers, is to shift from curricular sequences alone, to child-centered teaching from curricular frameworks, based on individual student abilities, learning characteristics, and data. Some of this individualized decision making occurs in planning decisions. But reading is a dynamic process, and some decisions about how to support and respond to learners during instruction occur in the moment. It was interesting and ongoing work for me to improve how to organize and support their teaching experience with one student for the semester. I was on site to get to know their students, and to coach and offer feedback during our class that followed the tutoring.

Though all candidates began with uncertainty and fear, nearly all grew through the semester and took risks to make decisions in their planning and teaching based on what they were learning about reading and their individual learners. My role was to guide and support, but also to leave room for their decision making. For example, when was their student ready for more challenging texts or higher skill levels in phonemic awareness and phonics instruction? How could each tutor's teaching and support allow each young student to take control of his or her reading process, and to experience appropriate levels of challenge and success? I was more likely to ask guiding questions to explore a candidate's thinking about next steps, without telling them exactly what to do. We used the language of "experimentation." If observations and data suggested a change, what would make sense? Why? Try it and pay attention. Adjust as needed.

But sometimes one or two candidates, for whatever combination of causes and conditions, struggled to take on the role of decision maker. Their instruction often did not match their student's abilities and needs, and their planning decisions seemed random and disconnected from their student's performance and their data. Either they did not seek any support from me, or they wanted a lot of support, in the form of "telling them exactly what to do." Guiding questions seemed to make them uncomfortable and even frustrated.

For me, this experience was grounded in two very strong intentions. First, I wanted to help all of my candidates to develop a strong foundation in teaching individualized developmental reading. Just as strong, my second intention was to do my best to ensure that students with disabilities and their families would have special educators who can deliver on the promise of IDEA (Individuals with Disabilities Education Act — federal education law for students with disabilities) and provide effective, individualized reading instruction, a critical need. My candidates, after all, had chosen a professional path to serve students with disabilities as special educators.

I needed to work with myself every week to keep showing up for the one or two candidates who were not progressing. It was unpleasant and difficult. I needed to stay present to both my intentions and to their learning needs.

As I became aware of this as a focus of my practice, I began to respond differently. First, I had to focus on clarifying my intention. I realized that my old focus on "everyone must learn to teach reading well" was my attachment to an *outcome*. I needed to accept that maybe I did not control all of the conditions that would always make that possible. This remained a course objective, and each candidate needed to demonstrate adequate understandings and performance to pass the course and move forward in the program. However, outcomes are not the same as intention.

Mindfulness helped me to sort this out. I came to clarify that while the professional standards remained high, my *intention* was to do my best as a teacher and mentor to create the best conditions I could that would support each candidate's potential success. My intention helped me to reflect on my responses and behaviors. My intention was about my own offering. It had nothing to do with the candidate's performance. Who did I want to be as teacher and mentor? I wanted to stay connected and present, even when things were not going well. I wanted to continue teaching and coaching, and to respond to each candidate in meaningful ways, based on where he or she was in the learning process. I wanted to be respectful and human and supportive. I also wanted to do this within the context of the defined standards of a professional development program. That is, I had to remain honest with myself and with the candidate about their progress in relation to the professional expectations. This was difficult practice. Each class, every week, I did my best to revisit my intentions before, during, and after written or live interactions with a struggling candidate. In the previous chapter I described a conference with a student, Anna, where I was able to be mindful and meet my intention.

It took more effort for me to remain connected to such a candidate. It took more time. I continued to revise more of my teaching behaviors to align with my intention. I didn't always get it right. But here are some of the kinds of behaviors that I tried on to honor my intention and maintain professional integrity. Before reading lesson plans and written work from a struggling candidate, I would be sure I was available. I would take a short break or read it early in my grading, while I was fresh. I would re-read and revise comments to be sure I was highlighting some strengths. I would reword comments and suggestions to be constructive. I would delete things that seemed too complicated and say, "Let's meet and talk this part through." But I would also leave room for their decision making and hold them to an appropriate standard for the work. I would create frequent opportunities for interaction, inviting them to meet even if they did not come forward. I would coach and explore from a decision-making frame. I would encourage some risks. I would applaud risks or some effort at decisions even if they did not work out. Sometimes, individuals still were not able to demonstrate beginning professional competency and did not pass the graduate class and field experience. I came to understand that there may be other causes and conditions for their lack of adequate progress at the time that were not in my control. My job was to make my best offering to create the conditions I could to support their success.

Mindfulness helped me to let go of the idea that a candidate's failure was my personal failure. But it also made me accountable for staying connected through my anxiety and discomfort and continuing to make my best offering as the teacher. And it helped me to recognize and own my unskillfulness when I did not meet my intention. When I did that, I often had to choose an action to acknowledge this and reconcile.

Beginning Anew: Owning and Responding to My Unskillfulness

Though my intentions are strong, and I try to practice diligently, I still sometimes get things very, very wrong. At times, this might be a brief, unskillful comment, which can be particularly difficult if made in the presence of others, such as responding to an individual in front of the class. Occasionally, I learn that I have been unaware of my part in an ongoing pattern that is causing suffering for a student or another individual. Let me share two examples.

One fall semester, during the initial weeks of the literacy class and clinic experience, I was working to manage my reactivity with a graduate student, Jennifer, who sometimes shared uninvited, irrelevant comments about students she knew who participated in our reading clinic. Jennifer frequently worked as a substitute teacher in this school. She was not yet very connected to graduate classmates, and perhaps nervous about her place in this graduate experience. Sometimes, I would overhear Jennifer, in the time before clinic, discussing students in a less than positive light with another candidate, who would also share negative stories about young learners whom she served in another district. I was aware of my irritation, but decided to ignore her comments, believing these might fade as she became more comfortable and gained confidence.

During one particular graduate class I was sharing a video sample of a tutoring session from a previous semester and prompting candidates to observe and identify early reading behaviors and abilities within their small groups. Jennifer knew this learner from subbing, and interrupted my guiding questions, calling out to the class that she knew and had worked with this student in the tape. I reacted immediately, calling her out in front of the class and directing her to focus on the activity's purpose of learning about the reading process. My tone was irritated and impatient. Her face fell in embarrassment. I saw the pain in her expression. The whole class fell silent. I was immediately aware of my reactivity. I paused briefly, then redirected everyone back to the guiding questions and we moved on.

After class, Jennifer hung back as others departed. I approached her and said, calmly and sincerely, "I am sorry I was unskillful in my response to you." She expressed her frustration, saying, "I am trying so hard, and everything I do is wrong." Her tone was not angry. I felt her vulnerability.

Somehow, the right words came to me. I was calm and looked her in the eye, speaking with assurance and kindness. "That's not how I see you. Your work so far has been very solid, especially your work with Nathaniel. Your lesson plans are well developed and a good match for his abilities and needs. Your teaching is very strong. From what I have seen so far, you belong here. You can succeed." I paused for a brief moment, watching her take this in, and added, again, "I am sorry I responded so unskillfully to you this evening."

What I said was true. Her planning and teaching were quite good. Though I had written positive comments and feedback to her each week on her assignments, she had continued to experience significant anxiety in class among peers. And I did feel deep regret for my reactivity. Most importantly, I was present and grounded as I said it.

I watched her face and her body relax. She thanked me. Something softened in me, and perhaps in her, too.

Though not formally planned, my comments reflected the first two steps in Beginning Anew, which is a practice I have received from the Plum Village tradition. This is a practice to reconcile when we have caused suffering, or when another has made us suffer. Sometimes, the process can be brief, and can happen immediately to right a wrong, as in the above example. What is important is that we are really present and vulnerable in the process, and not rushing through, sharing words to "get this over with" and relieve our embarrassment or anxiety.

The recommended frame for Beginning Anew practice has three steps (Nhat Hanh, 2010).

Step one: "Flower watering." We begin by sharing our appreciation for the other person. We talk about some of their strengths and positive characteristics that we appreciate. This must be authentic and reflect meaningful attributes.

Step two: Sharing regrets. The next step is to take responsibility for any ways we may have contributed to the problem, intentionally or unintentionally. We talk about any of our unskillful words or actions or thoughts that are relevant.

Step three: Expressing a hurt (if we are the one who was harmed or hurt by another's words or actions). We tell an individual how we felt hurt by an interaction because of unskillful words or actions or thoughts. (We only do this after the first two steps.)

In my brief interaction with Jennifer after class, I was able to respond with the first two steps from this process.

Step one: "*Flower watering*." My very honest comments about my perceptions of Jennifer's solid performance in her planning and teaching reflected this step.

Step two: *Sharing regrets*. My brief, grounded statement of apology for my unskillful reaction to her comment in class was a meaningful expression of my regret, taking responsibility for my part in this experience.

While there are three potential steps in Beginning Anew, each situation is unique. We discern how many steps might be a skillful match for a particular situation and partner. We reflect on all of the steps as we process our experience. Unless two individuals share a relationship (e.g., friends, ongoing colleagues) and are experienced mindfulness practitioners, it is recommended that we only implement the first one or two steps. Even if we are both experienced, we also consider the other person's capacity in this situation to participate in this process. We still may share only the first one or two steps. The first two steps seemed appropriate and came quite naturally in my interaction with Jennifer after class. I wanted her to hear and trust how I saw her performance, and my regret for the hurt I caused by my reactive comment. This is consistent with the purpose of Beginning Anew. It was not appropriate in this moment to tell her how I felt irritated when she occasionally made irrelevant comments in class or for the conversations I overheard before class. That might need to be discussed at another time. To bring up anything about her behavior as part of this interaction would likely make her feel criticized, which would make it impossible for her to hear or trust my ownership of my behavior and regret.

Sometimes, situations are more complex and require time to process and plan for Beginning Anew. We may have to practice and wait a day or more so that we can reflect on our experience and be present and open-hearted (vulnerable) in the process. I had another experience with a candidate one semester (as I was actively practicing) that was a painful reminder that my lack of mindfulness can cause great suffering.

This individual, Max, had learned that his mom, who had raised him as a single parent, had a life-threatening illness. She had been diagnosed at the end of the prior semester, 6 weeks before this semester began. His mom lived quite a distance from the college community. Max and I had not met prior to this semester. I was aware of his experience from my colleagues who had worked with him the previous semester. He was very close to his mom who had few other family supports. Max was devastated. Though other faculty who knew Max advised him that it would be fine to take the semester off to support his mom, or to attend graduate studies part time, he decided to return immediately to full-time graduate studies.

Max presented with great enthusiasm in the reading clinic practicum situation, in his interactions with me in class, and during individual conversations. He connected easily with his young student. He was also consistently late with submitting written lesson plans, and the quality of his plans and instruction was poor. While I asked candidates to post lesson plans a day ahead so I could support their thinking before they taught, I received his just hours before reading clinic. This prevented me from offering feedback ahead of time, so he could make adjustments before he taught the lesson. I fell into a pattern of giving tons of corrective guidance through coaching during his tutoring. I also offered a lot of individual suggestions to him during the grad class that followed. I had growing concerns about his lack of progress.

In retrospect, I think I hesitated to address his late lesson plans and limited performance explicitly because I knew of his personal suffering. When I tried to give more feedback verbally when we were together, he always responded well during our interactions, and said he welcomed the feedback — but his plans and teaching did not change much. Finally, with half of the semester behind us, he wrote me a painfully honest email about how he experienced my teaching: as constant and devastating criticism.

Firstly, I was shocked. I had no idea. It was so painful to learn this, and so far from who I wanted to be as his, or anyone's, teacher, I did not even make up stories in my head. I was deeply saddened to know that I had been adding to his suffering at a time in his life that was already extremely painful. As I looked back at my perceptions, I realized I had been avoiding an honest response to this candidate's under-preparation, incomplete work, and poor performance. This distancing with low performing students is an old pattern, but one I thought I had transformed as I worked with mindfulness. But knowing about Max's personal situation made me hesitant to initiate this hard conversation about his sub-par work and lack of progress.

I wanted to respond, but how? It came to me pretty quickly to apply Beginning Anew, first to process my own experience and then to think about how I might offer a sincere and skillful response.

> *To begin anew is to look deeply and honestly at ourselves, our past actions, speech and thoughts and to create a fresh beginning within ourselves and in our relationships with others." — Plum Village.org*

I needed some time to feel and process my experience. I allowed and stayed with my sadness about not meeting my intention for this already vulnerable candidate. Before we met, I used the Beginning Anew practice to reflect on my experience and to organize my thinking for my response. I wrote it out in detail for myself. Both the frame of this practice, and the writing helped me to stay connected on a human level to myself, and to the candidate. I invited Max to meet. Gratefully, he agreed. We met off campus, rather than in my campus office. I was clear that I needed to stay in touch with my own disappointment and vulnerability to ensure that I was authentic in this process. I shared all of the following face-to-face, in conversation.

You bring so many strengths as an educator. You are bright, enthusiastic, and very in tune with your student. From the beginning, you have been noticing and responding to Daniel holistically, closely monitoring his social-emotional experience, not just his academic learning. You notice and seamlessly make adjustments in the moment to respond to his signs of anxiety or frustration, which sometimes takes subtle forms, like fading out. You come in to assist or to infuse some light, playful energy to defuse tension. All of your interactions with Daniel are respectful, authentic, and encouraging. Your enthusiasm for creating opportunities for all learners to have rich, genuine experiences with texts is evident. This energy comes through with every conversation about texts that you share with him in your lessons.

These are qualities that are quite challenging for some teachers and pre-service teachers to develop. I have had some candidates every semester who understand the reading process and teaching strategies, but who struggle to connect with themselves and their student in meaningful ways. Though their teaching may be accurate, it is mechanical and lifeless. These characteristics are the most challenging aspects for me to "coach" someone in growing. I cannot overstate the importance of this foundational approach to seeing the learner and teaching from this relational stance. I think so much of it comes from how we see ourselves, and our willingness to be present to partner with learners in this process.

My self-assessment of our partnership this semester indicates that I have often not been successful in creating this learning context for you. I am now not surprised to read that you have often felt harshly criticized (not just in the last class). It makes sense that this would make you feel unsafe and tentative about asking questions. This is certainly not the learning context I want to create. I am well aware it is not conducive to supporting learning. Because I did not give you written feedback before you taught, I wound up doing a lot of corrective talk and modeling during your teaching with Daniel. I did often struggle with feeling I needed to address things the day they emerged. With half the semester gone, I regret that you have not had a positive and supportive learning experience — and worry that we don't have the time for me to shift that experience. I so appreciated your freshness and eagerness in learning about reading instruction when the semester began and looked forward to an exciting and fruitful journey. As the instructor, this is my responsibility to try to create and sustain this.

I have looked deeply into my part in this. I am trying to understand the roots of my reactivity that was triggered, to result in what you received as harsh criticism instead of supportive guidance. I should have spoken to you sooner and more explicitly about some of my growing frustration with the ways our shared experience was unfolding. Because I did not do this, I realize now that I was strengthening my fears and my anxiety would come out during class.

Let's see what we can do in the short time we have left to clarify and solidify your understandings of teaching reading to address your student's needs as a reader. I think you have much to offer as an educator. I believe you are capable of shifting your instruction to teaching that supports your student's reading process. I trust that some of the foundation you have from this semester will allow you to continue to grow this element of your teaching as a special educator.

This candidate was mature for his years, and he cared deeply about his teaching. I was very grounded and in touch with my own sadness about all of this as we spoke. My tone was steady and even, and I hope, kind and understanding. Our conversation was valuable, I think. Max seemed able to be present and to receive it.

The Beginning Anew practice provided a frame for an honest, vulnerable response to my unskillfulness. His work was consistently late and of poor quality. But I was the instructor, and one who was trying to do this work mindfully. I had to accept that I had failed to meet my intention with this individual and that, worse, I had caused him additional suffering during a very painful time. Sometimes the best we can do is respond as skillfully as possible when we get it wrong and take care to learn from it.

I continue to make sense of how to work with my unskillfulness with this practice. The purpose of Beginning Anew is to create a context for presence and listening, in order that mutual understanding can be achieved. In these examples, it is also about taking responsibility for my own actions when I don't meet my intention. It is not about being right or justified. I do not practice Beginning Anew with the expectation that the other person will forgive me, respond positively, or take any responsibility for their part in our difficulty. It is an offering from my heart. It is to remember and honor my intention and attempt to support conditions for our relationship in this shared work. That is not to say that we ignore other issues. For example, in my experience with Max, we needed to talk honestly about the quality of his work and the progress he needed to make to succeed in this course, even during this difficult time in his life.

But — big but here — I realized that a conversation about his behavior was not part of the Beginning Anew process. That would have shifted the attention from my behavior to his. I wanted him to hear me in the Beginning Anew conversation and know how much I appreciated him, how I heard and understood his pain, and how deeply I regretted my unskillfulness. I wanted him to know that I took responsibility for my actions that caused this pain. His habits and work and how these were impacting his progress was another conversation. Talking about his part in this problem would have made it difficult — perhaps impossible — for him to hear and trust my message about my own actions. Lerner (2017) offers guidance that I find relevant to the Beginning Anew process. She highlights why we need to be clear on the focus of these tough conversations and the need to schedule another time, or times, to explore other related issues. Often, we need more than one conversation to resolve bigger challenges.

Beginning Anew is a process to honor our humanity, our self-worth and the worthiness of others. My Beginning Anew process with Jennifer and with Max was about me being the person I wanted to be and expressing my wish to see and understand them as people, including their hurt. It is separate from my professional role and our relationship as teacher and student.

Max and I did meet again, as professor and student, and calmly discussed his work. I spoke calmly, clearly, and frankly about his work as it related to professional criteria. I stated that I was limited in my ability to support and guide him in this new learning when his plans were consistently late. He wound up making some very real shifts in his planning and teaching, and successfully completed the course and field experience. I was pleased we were able to connect as teacher and student to support his academic success. But it never felt like we recovered enough in the remaining weeks to have a trusting, caring relationship on a human level. He remained guarded in our informal interactions. I had to be okay with the way things were. Beginning Anew is not about me "getting" anything.

These examples provide considerations for how the practice of Beginning Anew can support our reflection and responses in situations when we are unskillful, or when there are conflicting perspectives or misunderstandings. Beginning Anew has been a very helpful frame for me to plan and engage in skillful interactions in many challenging situations. One of the critical elements of this practice is to be sure that I have the capacity to be present and solid during the Beginning Anew interaction, whether it is brief, as in my first example, or more complex, as in my second. If I am experiencing anger, frustration, or irritation, I know that I need to wait and practice mindfulness and use these steps to understand my experience before I have an interaction with the other person. My authentic presence — which is my vulnerability (with myself as well as my partner) — is the critical foundation for this practice of reconciliation.

These mindfulness practices (monitoring my stories, staying present in difficult conditions, Beginning Anew) have increased my sense of clarity about my teaching offering. Clarity supports my trust in my professional decision making. It is grounded in my growing professional knowledge, experience, and understanding. Mindfulness is the foundation of this clarity, which often emerges as insight, without intellectual pursuit or effort.

Clarity can feel empowering and energizing. It is the by-product of experiencing, and accepting, "*things are just the way they are.*" When reality reflects preferred conditions in my teaching life, I welcome this clarity — like when a candidate demonstrates informed, effective teaching; when I have a meaningful coaching interaction from a place of presence; when I have insight about how to respond to a complex advocacy situation. But clarity can also present in other, less inviting forms. Sometimes candidates do not demonstrate necessary competencies, in spite of my best efforts and theirs. Or sometimes, I leave a meeting or interaction with the heavy feeling that my anxiety took over, and that I was anything but a present, skillful teacher — and that I likely caused suffering. Because I am human and imperfect, and because there are many causes and conditions that I cannot control related to others' performance, these realities also continue to present sometimes.

Clarity means that I notice and cannot deny or ignore these less pleasant realities. Mindfulness is first about accepting that yes, "things are the way they are." If I am mindful, I must assess my part in these experiences and choose a skillful response that does not ignore or deny a reality that makes me uncomfortable.

My mindful teaching experiments unfolded and went deeper each semester over a number of years. I would sometimes write short pieces about my experiences, only for myself, as a way to reflect and process. Along the way, I occasionally shared short pieces with my writing group, because I trusted them deeply. Several years after my retirement, I began to draft a longer text to write about this experience for a broader audience. It was during that part of my writing process, when I was no longer teaching, that my central insights emerged. The chapters that follow (Part Three) discuss these insights, in the form of three elements that seem to be the foundational conditions that support my mindfulness in my teaching.

Part Three

Insights: Conditions That Support Mindfulness in My Teaching Work

In Part Three (chapters seven through nine), I discuss significant insights from my mindful teaching explorations. My mindful teaching experiences were connected to planning and teaching activities with a wide range of learners, across a variety of settings, from elementary schools to graduate classes at a public university. Insights emerged over time, supporting my growing understanding of this transformational period of my teaching career.

Insights: Conditions That Support Mindful Teaching

Insights about three conditions were present across contexts and learners. These factors, which emerged as most supportive to my mindful teaching experiences, relate to the teacher's awareness of:

- Professional knowledge, skills, and dispositions.
- Inner experiences: Cultivating awareness and skillful responses.
- Intention: Vision and compass for the journey.

In the chapters that follow, I share how these conditions, which were grounded in my experiences, inform my developing understanding of mindful teaching.

Chapter 7

Professional Knowledge, Skills, and Dispositions: Student Learning Matters

As a mindful teacher, I am still a teacher; someone who is, of course, accountable for all of my students' learning. I am recognizing how my professional preparation and ongoing professional development are conditions that support my ability to cultivate mindfulness in my teaching. This professional development path for me includes significant changes in my field of special education for interpreting disability, for developments in effective curricula and pedagogical practices, and for making learning accessible through a multitude of new and emerging technologies. My learning necessitated explorations beyond my field of special education, to learn about other frameworks and practices that are relevant for all educators, to be able to view my offering through a critical lens for learners of all ages. For example, a more recent development in my teaching career has been deepening my learning about how schooling is structured in relation to culture, language, race, class, gender, (dis)ability, and sexual identity. These understandings are necessary to identify and address (unknown) biases and barriers in my own teaching perceptions, actions, and content, and to help new teachers to develop a critical lens to inform their professional offering. My learning about how my teaching practices intersect with conditions that impact student learning (e.g., trauma-informed teaching practices, universal design for learning) are fundamental to supporting the success of all learners. This kind of broader and ever-growing professional knowledge supports my favorable professional dispositions and supports me to teach from a wise and informed understanding of conditions that shape my beliefs. This in turn makes me more mindful of the way such factors influence my impact on students, and helps inform my curricular choices, my practices, and my expectations for schooling.

Reflections on My Experience with Damien

As I revisited my individual session with Damien, a complex learner with autism whom I had never previously met, I thought about how much my professional knowledge, skills, and dispositions contributed to the successes we shared. I am a professional special educator. For nearly a decade, I taught in public schools, working with students of various ages who have disabilities. During that period, I earned a master's degree in my field. Then I returned to graduate studies, earned a doctorate with a focus on teaching students with disabilities, and co-developed and directed graduate programs in special education for 25 years. The field of special education changed rapidly during my 35-year professional career. We continue to learn about the capacities of people with disabilities, and about teaching practices, curricula, communication, and assistive technology that make learning accessible. In the West, there have been significant cultural shifts in how disability is perceived, as a result of de-institutionalization and community living reforms, the Disability Rights / Self Advocacy Movement, and the development of Disability Studies as a scholarly field. Nearly everything about my initial university preparation in special education thirty-some years prior was obsolete when I met Damien. The professional knowledge and skills I was able to offer in this session included:

- Professional knowledge about Developmental Literacy, particularly scaffolding and supporting emergent to early readers and writers to engage with and produce texts.
- Professional knowledge about how to use common technology tools for disability-related barriers to engage and support learners' active participation and success.

- Professional knowledge about effective teaching, adaptations, and support practices to engage and assist students with significant disabilities, including moment-to-moment decisions about increasing or reducing support and partnering to create and sustain an engaging pace and support success.
- Professional knowledge about autism and developmental disabilities to recognize signs of common characteristics, as well as skills to minimize the impact by preventing / minimizing difficulties and responding skillfully.
- Knowledge of new and growing evidence that many students with autism (and other disabilities) who cannot speak have far greater intellectual capacity than they can express without meaningful assistive technologies for communication. (Damien was presumed to have a significant intellectual disability and had no alternative / augmentative communication system.)
- My professional dispositions include respect (a "presumption of competence"), as well as advocacy, collaboration, and authentic learning. I saw my "evaluation" work as exploring conditions that would support Damien's access to meaningful instruction and maximize his learning opportunities. It was my job to find out what knowledge, tools and practices his **teachers** needed to support his success, not to confirm others' perceptions of his incompetence. Our session was a time for me to try out things based on the question, "What might I do if I were Damien's teacher? What learning conditions can I create **with** him? What kinds of interesting materials, tools and practices might invite and support his participation?" Below is part of a reflection I wrote about my time with Damien when I was trying to analyze why our session worked. My focus at that time was on my professional knowledge and skills (not yet considering the impact of mindfulness).

When I met Damien, I had been teaching a graduate reading course for special education candidates for a number of years. This course included a reading clinic (tutoring experience) for each graduate student, twice a week, with an elementary learner who had a "mild" disability (e.g., a learning disability) and who demonstrated delays in learning to read. This clinic was an integral part of a graduate course on specialized reading practices for students with disabilities. I was always present for reading clinic to supervise and coach my graduate students' experience. I knew that this clinic experience with 25 new graduate students and 25 new elementary learners each semester was significantly impacting my professional development. It was continually challenging, broadening, and deepening my understandings about developmental literacy and the reading process, and effective practices for teaching early readers who struggle. I trusted my developmental literacy foundation.

During our session, I drew upon my professional knowledge of literacy in a number of ways. I invited Damien to join me in authentic reading and writing experiences. I wanted to provide opportunities for him to engage with interesting content and materials, particularly after viewing the meaningless isolated tasks that made up much of his school day. I read continuous texts to him, and we co-constructed short pieces through shared writing about a topic, rather than working only with isolated words or letters. My understandings of shared reading and shared writing, often utilized with emergent literacy learners, allowed me to envision and facilitate Damien's active participation in meaningful reading and writing processes as my partner, with varying types of support. Damien did not speak and had no alternate communication system (other than a handful of signs). But we could and did engage with shared reading and writing. My clinic experience, where we served many early readers and a few emergent readers each year, informed my ability to scaffold and support Damien's participation in literacy explorations with texts.

I looked for ways to invite and allow Damien to be in control of his reading and writing as much as possible. When we viewed the first digital text on the laptop and he reached for the space bar, I supported and then allowed him to advance after we read each page. I presented choices as often as possible for him to decide what to write about (e.g., __ or crab), what to read about (e.g., dolphins or sharks), and what facts to include in his writing (e.g., Dolphins eat fish. Dolphins breathe air). Choices conveyed respect, rather than control, and invited more agency on his part.

I chose informational topics and texts that I thought would be more engaging and age-appropriate for a 12-year-old boy. While I provided a high level of support, the literacy strategies and accommodations I offered came directly from effective practices for all literacy learners. For example, because Damien could not read the text aloud to me, I structured the last reading activity with a focus on comprehension strategies. We previewed the text selection (dolphins) and pictures, and I constructed a graphic organizer highlighting what we would read about (i.e., dolphin life, how dolphins breathe, kinds of dolphins). We "chunked" the text into shorter sections, and I specified the focus for the passage before and after reading (i.e., how dolphins breathe). We took notes after each section, adding text-based facts to the graphic organizer. We re-read the list of notes for each section of the graphic organizer, and all of the notes after reading, to summarize what we learned.

Similarly, writing strategies and supports also came from professional knowledge and experiences with literacy instruction. We used the shared reading about dolphins as a springboard for writing. Writing must come from one's knowledge or experience. We used the shared text to build background knowledge to write a short piece about dolphins. Pre-writing support is essential for early and striving writers. We used the graphic organizer to organize the writing. Damien made choices from the notes on the graphic organizer to decide what to include in his writing. ("What do you want to say about dolphin life? Live in groups or eat fish?") This was a very basic experience of writing an informational text using another text as a resource. The text we co-constructed through shared writing was also a written summary of the text excerpt we read together.

I had never implemented reading or writing instruction with a student who had characteristics like Damien's. Here was a student with autism who did not speak, was described as having a significant intellectual disability, and who was best known for his "intense challenging behaviors." I have spent a fair amount of time with students with such characteristics, and in past lives learned and wrote about alternate curricula and functional skills. I knew these were no longer defensible, as the professional literature was documenting how technology could support communication and literacy learning for students like Damien. But I had no experience teaching reading and writing to students with such complex disabilities.

However, on this day, I did not focus on Damien's "differences." My growing professional frame of reference was literacy — and how to help all students participate as readers and writers. The lens that I brought to working with Damien that day was to understand him as a literacy learner. As I re-read the field notes, I realized that my growing professional knowledge and skills from my ongoing work, preparing teachers to teach literacy, and especially the clinic experience, were readily available to inform my shared reading and writing experiments with Damien. Of course, my professional knowledge continues to change and grow. Based on my current experience, today I would share more sophisticated texts with Damien, and explore additional formats (e.g., print and digital).

Professional Knowledge of Disability-Related Characteristics

My knowledge and experience as a special educator also informed my experience with Damien, encouraging me to look at the big picture as I observed him and thought about his behavioral challenges. The fact that he could not speak and had no reliable communication system made me wonder about his teacher's assumptions about his intellectual abilities. I noticed that his body seemed tense and rigid, and that his movements seemed random at times. I knew many students who had autism who also experienced sensory integration issues. Damien's schedule included no sensory breaks or programmed sensory input.

I wondered how many of his "aggressive behaviors" represented attempts to communicate and / or his responses to his unmet sensory needs. As I viewed his isolation from his classmates, spending most of his day with a teaching assistant and being prodded through short segments of mundane tasks for meaningless "work," I was curious if his behavior and disengagement were connected to the dearth of meaningful learning activities and interactions. Could his behaviors be attempts to communicate his frustration and boredom? Best practices in special education had shifted to interpreting challenging student behaviors through a holistic and educative lens.

Professional knowledge and experience as a special educator also informed my moment-to-moment decisions about how to support Damien in ways that might minimize the impact of some disability-related challenges (e.g., unmet communication, sensory integration needs) and sustain his engagement. Even when working in very early literacy activities, I spoke to Damien in a calm, age-appropriate tone, one that conveyed that I presumed his competence. And while I was clearly the leader-facilitator, I spoke and structured interactions in ways that were based on a shared partnership, rather than directing him through tasks or steps to be done "on his own" or "for me."

Because Damien and I did not have a shared communication system, I used a lot of visual formats to structure and support our reading, writing, and interactions. My experience with students who have autism also indicates that many prefer and benefit from visual input, rather than only auditory information. I pointed or helped him point, tracking the text as I read aloud. I previewed the visual layout and buttons on the whole word writing software, while modeling how it worked, and while supporting his choices. I wrote choices on the whiteboard for him to point to (e.g., fish or mammal, yes or no). I showed him relevant pages with illustrations in the book about animals when I asked what he wanted to read about (dolphins or sharks). I constructed a graphic organizer section by section as a pre-reading tool. I spoke aloud as I wrote key words, so he could see the visual emerging; I pointed to the words as we previewed topics and reviewed notes. When Damien was constructing sentences about dolphin facts, I wrote possible sentence starters and word choices on the whiteboard; first for him to choose from, and then for him to copy, to support his memory and spelling as he typed.

When Damien grew restless and moved around, I suspected sensory integration needs (rather than assuming avoidance, non-compliance, or aggression). I offered sensory input first (pressure on his shoulders, brushing his arms), and when that was not helpful enough, I offered him a short break.

When Damien attempted physical movements that seemed uncoordinated, I presumed these were intentional. I know that many people with autism experience motor planning difficulties, and that fine motor actions are particularly challenging. I supported his forearm and encouraged him to hit the space bar to turn the "pages" of our digital book; I helped him isolate his index finger and supported his hand above the keyboard, allowing him to choose the letters as he typed.

Rather than focusing on how to respond to challenging behaviors, I experimented with practices to minimize problem behaviors from occurring, and to support his engagement in meaningful learning to practice desired behaviors. I tried to offer meaningful, high interest activities (e.g., using laptop, exploring information texts). I created a visual schedule to preview and talk through our sequence of activities, so he knew what we were going to do. I supported authentic shared reading and writing of continuous texts about interesting, age-appropriate topics, offering choices of what to write about, what to read about, and what to include in his writing piece. When he began moving around a lot in his chair and moving his arms, I offered sensory input and then, a short break.

I was also conscious of supporting Damien's participation in ways that sustained his engagement. My talk was encouraging and instructional, rather than framing things as a test, where his attempts would be judged as "right" or "wrong." When he did not respond, I could, as his partner, share information and build background knowledge ("I wonder if you know this, Damien. ... Whales are actually mammals. They breathe air like us"). I varied my supports, offering more help when he hesitated or did not respond, modeling, teaching, helping, in order to keep the experience of authentic shared reading and shared writing going. As the leader and facilitator, I created a meaningful, shared pace and flow through my teaching, prompts and supports, rather than letting things grind to a halt if he did not (could not) respond.

While my knowledge and skills were not the "whole story" regarding the magic Damien and I experienced in that session, I feel certain that, no matter how grounded and mindful I was, without my professional competence as a special educator, we would have had little or no success. In an earlier chapter, I reported this insight: "My only job is to monitor myself in order to maintain my own mindfulness. When I can do that, *and am engaged in something within my capacity*, much of the rest can often just flow." The quality of my professional development makes this possible in teaching moments as they unfold; it determines a critical piece of my capacity.

Reflections on My Experience with Graduate Special Education Candidates

My professional knowledge and skills also were critical to informing program planning, instruction and coaching in graduate courses and field experiences. My teaching of adult learners in our graduate special education program required a clear understanding of the roles of these professionals in schools, including the competencies required by National Accreditation standards and for state certification. For example, the ability to provide specialized instruction in developmental reading is a critical competency for special educators. I wrote major revisions to our graduate program to add a six-credit course and field experience in specialized reading instruction.

The reading methods course and the tutoring element were completely integrated. Course assignments were based on candidates' application of their growing professional knowledge as it related to their work with their individual student. Assignments reflected key special educator competencies, such as:

- Implementing and interpreting various reading assessments.
- Monitoring student progress each week.
- Planning and providing data-based instruction matched to their learner's changing abilities.
- Assessing a student's overall literacy program, including general and special education sessions.

Because the reading methods course objectives were based on professional competencies in assessment, instruction, and program planning for students with reading difficulties, candidate assessment in this methods experience was based on performance assessments in these areas, as related to their work with their assigned student tutee.

My colleague and I also chose to supervise all of our candidates in their full-time internship placements. This allowed us to continue to monitor, coach, and support the application of knowledge and skills from prior methods courses and field experiences as they served many students with disabilities as a special educator within a public-school team. All of my program planning, course planning, instruction, and assessments were informed by my professional knowledge and skills as they related to competencies and expectations for special educators. This professional knowledge continued to grow and change as new research and practices in special education continued to emerge.

My dispositions were also clearly reflected in our master's program and my teaching decisions. The master's and doctoral programs I had graduated from were both deeply rooted in what would become a Disability Studies framework. I learned to recognize the injustice and negative impact of policies and practices that marginalized and segregated people with disabilities. I saw first-hand some of the benefits of early inclusive education programs and conducted research on limited mainstreaming programs. What my graduate studies did not offer was any help to ensure powerful learning for students with disabilities in inclusive education programs. While I believed deeply in the right of all students to be full and valued members of mainstream classes and schools, I was still a special educator. I wanted to prepare special educators who were committed to, and would bring the skills for, maximizing meaningful learning for students with disabilities in inclusive programs. I also felt, just as strongly, that as special educators they must be well prepared to ensure that all of their students maximize their capacities in critical areas such as literacy, curricular participation and learning, positive social skills and behaviors, and other individual priorities.

This advocacy disposition for both inclusion and meaningful learning guided both program and course decisions. Our special education foundations class (initial semester) taught about disability history and special education through a critical lens consistent with Disability Studies. It also required candidates to apply Universal Design for Learning principles to plan or revise a general education unit and sample lessons. We wanted candidates to commit to both a disposition that viewed students with disabilities as learners and to growing their teaching skills to maximize accessibility to the general education curriculum. All of our methods courses (literacy, positive behaviors, severe disabilities) provided examples of how special educators could implement individualized instruction and support within inclusive education classes. Assignments required candidates to create individual plans and discuss how to enact these in the context of inclusive general education settings (e.g., intensive reading instruction, behavioral interventions). We placed interns only in inclusive public school programs. In addition to specialized individual and small group instruction, we included requirements for teaming with general educators who shared responsibility for students with disabilities.

This insight about professional knowledge and skills reminded me that this condition supports and interacts with my mindfulness practice. Student learning is a part of mindful teaching. Mindfulness helps me to see things as they are, including my own true capacities and limitations. This helps me to recognize where I can continue to grow, both professionally and in my practice.

Chapter 8

Inner Experiences: Cultivating Awareness and Skillful Responses

It takes practice to cultivate real awareness — for most of us in this Western culture, daily practice. Meditation and other mindfulness practices were critical for me to learn to pay attention to changing experiences in my body and mind. I understood (intellectually) how mindful awareness might enhance my teaching, but I needed a daily meditation practice (outside of my teaching) to become more in tune with my inner experience through the day. This was the first step: to become curious and observe my body sensations, thoughts, and feelings during meditation. Only with that experience could I grow my capacity to begin to notice these in my teaching life, and to more often choose skillful responses when my inner experience became challenging. Daily meditation was how I built that foundation, and how I continue to strengthen and sustain it.

Mindfulness

By mindfulness, I mean being aware of what is happening in this moment — the present moment, both within me and around me. I continue to develop my ability to distinguish my actual experience from any feelings or stories I may have about what is happening. This includes practicing to observe my inner experience (i.e., physical sensations, emotions, thoughts), with kind, or at least neutral, observation. My inner experience is made up of my awareness of my body and its sensations, as well as thoughts and emotions that arise. Mindfulness is always mindfulness of something. I practice in my morning meditation to bring attention to my body, or my emotions or my thoughts, to grow my mindfulness of my inner experience. Focusing my daily practice in this way continues to build my awareness of my inner experience in daily life, including my teaching.

Mindfulness of Body

My first practice experiments were with mindfulness of the body. Yoga practice invited me to bring attention to the breath for meditation, pranayama (guided breath work), and asana (poses), moving through and holding different postures with focus. Singing and chanting on mindfulness retreats and at yoga classes / events were also body practices I experienced that engaged my breath and vocal cords. My body felt more regulated after these community experiences with breath, sound, and rhythm.

Based on my early reading, I began sitting in stillness each day, trying to keep my focus on my in-breath and my out-breath. When thoughts arose, I tried to let them go and not explore or engage with them. The instruction was to bring my attention back to the breath as my anchor and let thoughts fade or be in the background. In subsequent years, I learned about and tried other anchors in addition to breath. I may sit still and listen to all the changing sounds in the environment, keeping my focus tuned primarily on sounds. Or I may focus on ever changing sensations that come and go in my body, simply noting them, without judgment or an agenda. I may notice how a sensation changes from moment to moment (e.g., if it is increasing or fading, tingling, steady or pulsing). Other practice friends have shared with me that breath is not the anchor for them, and that it can even cause anxiety. This helped me to realize there is no one way to begin or grow one's practice.

For another body practice I have learned, I pause and check in with each of my senses. I tune into my environment in this moment, noticing what I see, what I hear, what I smell, what physical sensations I feel (e.g., contact with floor or seat, temperature), and what I taste. Just a moment or two for this multi-sensory check-in grounds me in my body and my setting, in the here and now. This is a wonderful outdoor practice for tuning in to natural surroundings such as the sounds of birds or rain, or wind in the trees, the sight of the sky and clouds, the feeling of the earth beneath me or the breeze, and the scent of flowers or mud or water.

As I began attending retreats and practicing with a community, I participated in more body-focused practices. These included guided body scans (Deep Relaxation), to invite my body into a calm state. I was instructed to bring attention to one body part at a time, usually moving up or down my body. I also learned how to practice walking meditation, letting go of thinking and bringing deep attention to every step and the movement of my body. Mindful eating during silent meals taught me to slow down for part or all of a meal or snack. I now notice the appearance and scent of my food. I take one bite at a time and chew thoughtfully, noticing the movement of my jaw, the flavors and textures of the food, the sensation of swallowing, pausing between bites. This engages multiple senses and allows me to be present for my food and appreciate it.

All of these mindful body practices help my mind and body to connect. When body and mind are one, I am able to be here in my life in the present moment. I am not lost in thoughts about the past or the future or "living in my head."

Mindfulness of Thoughts

My mind, like the minds of many others in our culture, is conditioned to engage with non-stop thinking. When I began to experiment with stopping and focusing on my breath or another anchor for even 5 minutes, my thoughts continued to interrupt my focus, demanding my attention. The instruction I received from books and recorded teachers was not to "stop" the thoughts, but to acknowledge them and try to return the focus to the anchor (e.g., breath, sound, sensations). I was encouraged to do this with kindness and instructed not to view these intrusions as an interruption to mindfulness, but rather to see their inevitable appearance, and the subsequent return to the anchor, as the core of mindfulness itself. No matter how many times thoughts showed up to interrupt, noticing and returning to my anchor *was* practicing mindfulness. Each time I noticed and came back, I was strengthening my "muscle of awareness." Sometimes a thought came in and, before I even noticed, a full-length movie was being projected in my mind. Still, the instruction was, whenever I noticed – whether it played for 5 seconds or 5 minutes – to simply and kindly come back to my anchor, and begin again. It often felt like a lively competition between my anchor and my thoughts.

My daily practice gives me a front row seat to notice what my thoughts are about. Very often my thinking is about the past, replaying conversations or experiences from the previous day, week, or from decades ago. These can be wholesome memories of a kind exchange or a tender moment. But more often for me, especially when I first began practicing, I became aware of how much time I spent replaying difficult memories. These included painful interactions or situations that had made me feel judged, fearful, angry, embarrassed, or disrespected. I began to see how a brief thought about a person or place that popped up could quickly spin into a complex story filled with my analysis, interpretations, opinions, and judgments, usually about others. My thoughts can also be about the future. These are mostly about anxieties in my current life such as health issues, family concerns, pending changes. For me, this kind of future worry often focuses on detailed action plans for how I can get more control over an (unknown) future scenario. My stories can fixate on the worst possible scenario, ignoring the fact that I have no idea what will happen in the future. Once a theme emerges, if I engage with it, it seems to revisit me often, for weeks or even months.

The more I practice stopping for quiet meditation each day, the more I can "catch" my thoughts before they become a full-blown story. And when I do engage with some story time, I tend to notice it sooner and let it go before it gets a lot of momentum. Noticing the content of my thoughts helps me to be aware when a challenging thought emerges (e.g., fear about a possible health issue), and actively invite my mind to replace that thought with a more helpful one (e.g., "Thank you for your opinion, my dear mind. I have access to great doctors and in this moment, I feel fine"). After this interruption of negative thinking, I can return to my anchor, repeating this as often as necessary in a single session.

Mindfulness of Emotion

My emotions are completely intertwined with my bodily sensations and my thoughts. It was very helpful for me to begin to realize that emotions are experienced first as energy in my body. A growing foundation of mindfulness of the body helps me to notice when feelings arise, both during meditation and, sometimes, during teaching. I may become aware of changes in my breathing, heat in my face, tension in my jaw or neck, or a feeling of speeding up in my speech or movements. This is my first step in practicing with *mindfulness of emotions*. Over time my reading and various teachers expanded my vocabulary for describing physical sensations. What was I experiencing in this part of my body as I was trying to be still and focus on my anchor? Was it tingling, pressure, heat or cold, pulsing, or something else? This helps me to bring focus to the physical sensation and name it in a descriptive way that can slow my reaction to it. If I can stay with it as a witness during meditation, I can explore which emotion is arising and presenting as this physical experience. With more experience, I found resources that also offered more extensive and specific vocabulary for a wide range of emotions, such as Brene Brown's list of *87 Human Emotions and Experiences* that emerged in her research (2023). Sometimes stopping and being quiet in meditation makes space for emotions to arise. When I can tune in to the body sensations in a descriptive way and stay with them, the emotion that is presenting more often reveals itself (e.g., fear, joy, anger, sadness, relief). Just recognizing, naming, and allowing the emotion, even for a minute or two, can often reduce its energy. I am more familiar now with the kinds of physical sensations I experience with certain emotions. Fear causes my heart rate to speed up, my jaw to tighten, my arm and leg muscles to tense in ways that make my movements faster and jerky; my voice pitch and volume increase and my speech speeds up. Love and gratitude create a sense of warmth and opening in my chest, my muscles are loose, muscles in my face and jaw feel soft, my breath is slow, and my eyes get a little teary.

My challenges are with the difficult emotions. The more I can notice body sensations that are connected to my emotions during meditation, the more opportunities I get to know those emotions and help them to settle.

Before I had practices and tools to recognize and practice with strong emotions, I was constantly pulled around by them, and often quite reactive. My emotions may first emerge as physical sensations (whether or not I notice), but in a flash my thoughts can join the dance to generate all kinds of stories to support and intensify the emotion. The more those stories run amok in my mind, the more frequently those emotions tend to arise, and the more likely I am to believe them. An emotion can arise (e.g., fear, embarrassment), a story can emerge (this person is to blame! Everything is ruined). Next, the emotion is stronger and driving my thoughts – and often, my speech and actions. This can still happen for me, but it is far less frequent, less intense, and I can recognize it soon after and reset my thinking. I am less likely to strengthen a story by ruminating about it for days and weeks. Practicing with noticing emotions, along with their accompanying physical sensations and thoughts during quiet daily meditation, is critical for me. The more I do this, the more these patterns begin to let go a bit. As I practice over time with my inner experience in meditation, I notice I can more often recognize the physical signs and common strong emotions in daily life, including my teaching. This recognition can support me to choose a different response when challenges pop up, instead of reacting or freezing.

For example, instead of blaming (e.g., naming my challenging student as the cause of the difficulty), I might be able to focus on my inner experience, my strong emotion ("There it is again, anger"). I need to know it and own it, if I am to transform it. The more I practice with naming and being and staying with strong emotions during meditation, the more I grow my capacity to not let these feelings pull me out of the present when they arise during my teaching work. This is very challenging, even on the cushion. But with practice, I am growing.

But here's the thing. Returning to presence does not mean the physical sensations of the feeling are gone immediately. It rarely happens that quickly. Even when I do a settling practice, such as breathing, the sensations in my body from that feeling do not immediately disappear. The practice of recognizing, naming, and *allowing* the strong emotion is very important to my foundation. I trust that my practice on the cushion will increase my ability to stay present in my teaching *while I may still be feeling uncomfortable sensations in my body* that were triggered by feelings. I am growing my capacity to learn to stay present to both the feeling and my teaching. The feeling usually does subside after a few minutes as I settle back into my teaching. When I have caved in to the strong pull to escape the feeling and was not able to stay with it, I notice that I lost my presence to myself and my students, and sometimes reacted with unskillful speech.

I am learning that I may need to return to that strong emotion and hold it later during a break or after school (without the stories), tending to it a little more. But I cannot stop my lesson for 20 minutes of belly breathing right now. When successful, I can notice and acknowledge the feeling, care for it in the moment with some breath, and *allow the sensation* as I get back to my work of teaching or the meeting at hand. When I do not acknowledge it and offer it some care, the strong emotion can shape my actions and interactions in unskillful ways (like when I lost my way in my consultation with young Misha, as I shared in chapter three). Or I may push it down, feeding stories and strong resentment that will limit my presence in the situation in the future and fuel more unintended unskillful actions. Choosing mindfulness often means I choose to tolerate some of the feeling during teaching, just as I do during my meditation. Because I recognize it and know it is there, I am less likely to be overwhelmed by the feeling and lose touch with myself, becoming reactive or disconnected.

Reflections on My Experiences with Students

The day I spent with Damien reflected the full range of inner experiences. My travel included a long flight, and I was physically very tired. My body, however, was charged up, and I had slept very little the night before. I was experiencing a lot of fear about this completely unstructured work where I would visit a different special education class each day and provide on-the-spot consultation and recommendations for a student the teacher found most challenging. Damien's school would be my first stop. My anxiety was off the charts. I was very aware of how it manifested physically. My stomach was "off," and felt semi-nauseous. I nibbled saltine crackers and sipped ginger ale and tea. My breathing was shallow and fast. My muscles were tense and felt weak. I felt cold, though the room's temperature was normal.

I recalled how I had felt so vulnerable on that trip, and particularly the morning before I visited Damien's school. My personal daily meditation practice had been in place for more than a year. That morning, due to my escalating anxiety, I spent more than my typical time with mindfulness practices, including sitting and walking meditation and listening to a recording of a meditation teacher's talk.

After my day with Damien, I was equally aware of how my body was so settled as we became engaged with our shared text explorations. I don't recall awareness of my stomach feeling better or my heart rate slowing. I replayed the session, seeing and feeling again that my movements and my speech were much slower and coordinated with his responses. I realized that I was not consciously trying to slow down. I recalled that during my time with Damien, my mind was clear and focused without effort. I knew I felt tired when I left the school, but it was a "good tired." I was grounded in my body, like the satisfying tired I might feel after a challenging yoga class.

And then there was a new opportunity with Misha a few months later.

My time with Misha could not have been more different than my time with Damien. I had great difficulty engaging her and sustaining her participation. I felt my frustration rising. I became rigid and increasingly controlling as I tried to steer "our" experience toward my imagined session. Some moments deteriorated completely into a power struggle between me and this 8-year-old child. We found no flow, no connection.

Even as I write this years later, I can feel the tension in my face and shoulders and strain in the front of my neck (vocal), as I see and feel my efforts to control this child's participation, trying to make things go according to my script. What were these physical feelings about? For me, I know now that experiencing old feelings of powerlessness and fear can manifest as control in many kinds of situations.

As previously mentioned, one of my patterns that I chose to focus on in my mindful teaching of my graduate students was the anxiety I experienced for candidates who were demonstrating limited progress. When a candidate was not doing well, I suffered a lot with *"the way things were."* Even reading their work online made my body tense and tight. My muscles wanted to move. It was hard to stay in my chair and continue reading or writing feedback. Stories would come up, often about blame. As previously noted, if a candidate consistently posted underdeveloped lesson plans or did not make changes related to my feedback, I might begin to have thoughts that *"She doesn't care about her student's learning"* or *"She is not putting effort into this course and field experience."* I realized my discomfort made me want to distance myself from this candidate.

As my practice helped me to recognize and practice with my emotions, I could try to let go of stories and apply practices to calm my body. The anxiety still came up but I decided to experiment with mindfulness to work with myself every week to keep showing up for them as individuals. It was unpleasant and difficult. It never got easier. But I recognized that my responsibility was to practice with the difficulty while maintaining integrity for professional standards. Anna, whose conference I shared in chapter five, was part of this experiment with myself.

That afternoon, before our conference, I practiced mindfulness to get myself grounded... I knew I would have to self-monitor for presence and manage my anxiety. I needed to keep my focus on me and my internal experience.... (During the beginning of our meeting) Anna offered very rote responses that did not align with her videotaped lesson or my observations... She mentioned something about her tutee's short attention span in a negative way. It sounded like she was blaming him and his attention difficulties, as an excuse or reason for his inconsistent engagement. Though this "blaming the student" is a hot button for me (and I feel some tension begin to rise in my neck and shoulders), I remained calm. I went on with this without judgment.

Sometimes, things come up in the moment that can touch difficult emotions. There is no time to reflect and plan and practice before an unexpected interaction. This can still happen for me. There were certainly times, when something occurred during a class or a meeting, that I did not recognize a body sensation connected to a difficult emotion and was reactive. Such was the case in my experience with Jennifer that I described in chapter six.

I was aware of my need to manage my reactivity with a graduate student, Jennifer, who sometimes shared uninvited, irrelevant comments during a full group class activity. These comments would move the focus away from the learning activity (e.g., looking at videotape together to analyze student reading behaviors). Sometimes, I would overhear Jennifer (who subbed in this school) discussing students who were in our tutoring program in a less than positive light with another candidate. I was aware of my irritation, but decided to ignore her comments, believing these might fade as she became more comfortable and gained confidence. One evening during class, Jennifer called out saying something irrelevant about a student who was in a tape we were viewing as a class. I reacted immediately, calling her out in front of the class and directing her to focus on the activity's purpose of learning about the reading process. My tone was harsh and short. The silence that fell over the class made it clear that my reactivity landed on every person in the room. It happened so quickly that I had no awareness of a body sensation before I spoke. I do clearly remember how my body felt immediately after my reactive comment. I felt tight in my face and my throat and my chest. I felt warmth spread across my face and then heat on my back and under my arms. The emotion connected to these physical sensations was one I could name: shame. It was difficult to experience, especially since the whole class had witnessed my unkind response. But I think that awareness of my body in the moments after that unskillful comment allowed me to let go of shame and to stay with embarrassment and regret. I did not get defensive; I felt embarrassed. We moved on, though the group energy was impacted for the rest of the class. Because I felt and named the shame, I was able to let it go, accept regret, and connect with Jennifer after class to reconcile.

Important Consideration

I want to share a very important final note here regarding mindfulness of our inner experience. Several years after I had retired from my faculty position, the context of much of this exploration, I began learning about Trauma Sensitive Mindfulness. This included developing new understandings of how the nervous system works, and so much more about how this shapes our inner experience. I also learned practices in addition to those I have shared here for caring for the nervous system to stretch my capacity for the unexpected without becoming overwhelmed. It is beyond the scope of this text to include this important information, since it was not part of my experience with mindful teaching.

However, today, when I introduce mindfulness practices or facilitate with experienced practitioners in other settings, I share basic information about the nervous system and do my best to use trauma sensitive facilitation practices. I know now that for some individuals who have a history of trauma, traditional mindfulness practices can be seriously triggering. Given my new learning, I consider trauma sensitive mindfulness understandings and practices to be an important foundation. Two resources that have supported my learning on this topic as a mindfulness practitioner and facilitator are the book *Unshakeable* by Jo-Ann Rosen (2023, Parallax Press) and Dr. Larry Ward's online, self-paced course *Earthgate* (n.d., Deeper Still Academy).

Chapter 9

Intention: The Heart of Mindful Teaching

Mindfulness of intention honors the people and experiences that watered my seeds of aspiration to become an educator, and it supports my journey to remain on a wholesome teaching path. My intention connects me to my teacher roots, and guides all of my teacher decisions, large and small. It reminds me of who I aspire to be in this work and of my responsibilities to my students and others as an educator. Intention supports my effort to maintain integrity in the many ways I make this offering. This is another dimension of mindful awareness. I reconnect with and try to follow a wholesome intention to grow and offer my best teacher-self in my service as an educator. As I became aware of intention in my mindful teaching explorations, I discovered that it flows from these two questions:

- Who do I aspire to be as a teacher?
- How do I want to impact my students' learning, now and in the future?

A new insight arose: mindful teaching is rooted in my wholesome intention, the heart of my inner teacher. This intention was nourished by experiences and people who inspired me and helped me to find my way to this path. Some teachers I know were aware of this very early. They cannot recall a time when they did not aspire to be a teacher. Others could identify a special person or time when they seemed to awaken to this understanding that their purpose is to teach. I think of the people who inspired and supported my journey to teaching as a kind of ancestor. I think for many of us, there are others who have been part of our path who are also teaching ancestors. These may be wonderful teachers we learned from as children and young adults. They may be mentors who were not professional educators, who touched us in ways that awakened a passion in us and helped us to experience the power of a caring, skilled teacher. Some may be gifted teachers from other times and places who we met through books or stories that capture the heart and spirit of their work.

One of my important teacher ancestors is my Uncle Bill, a Roman Catholic priest who was a founding faculty member, and later principal, of a diocesan boys' high school. I was decades into my career before I understood our connection. He was very close to my mother (his sister) and a significant presence through my childhood. Decades after my uncle's death, while I was emptying out a family file cabinet, I came across what must have been an old yearbook print of him. He was in his classroom standing in front of the blackboard, smiling into the camera. This image brought up a long-forgotten memory of the only time I had visited my uncle's classroom. I was a college student and was taking a psychology class. I needed a group of adolescents to take a brief survey for a course project. My uncle volunteered his students. Here is part of what I wrote about that memory, which is something I would read each year to my new teacher candidates.

I don't remember what the survey was about. I don't remember what I said to introduce it or what the results were when I tallied the responses.

What I remember, clearly, is my uncle, and what I witnessed about him that day in his classroom. This was his space. It seems now it was a sacred space; one where he was most himself — as teacher.

I remember clearly how he welcomed me and beamed when he introduced me to his students as his niece — the one who was studying to become a **teacher**. *And I recall how he glowed as he introduced his students to me. The love and the pride that he had for each of us was tangible in those moments.*

Teaching was his passion. It was the thing he was meant to do to make his contribution. It was a magical moment for me — witnessing this person who I had known my whole life as family, seeing him for the first time in his professional world; and touching a bit of my future.

My uncle died young, before he was 60. I think of him often when I reflect on my teaching life. I like to believe that I am his continuation in the world as the only teacher in my family of my generation. I know that teaching matters. I know it is the thing that I am meant to do to make my unique contribution.

My mother, his closest sibling and favorite sister, would often say to me as my teaching career unfolded: "Your uncle would be so proud. He loved teaching."

At first, I was disappointed that my uncle and I never got to have conversations about teaching, our shared passion. I was just beginning my career when he died. But as I continued in my mindfulness practice, I realized my uncle was still with me. I talk to him, especially when preparing for challenging teaching situations, like the last time I offered a very content-rich half-day workshop. I would invite him to ride with me, to breathe with me before I entered the space. I asked him to stay connected to me and help me to stay grounded, present to make my best offering. I can feel his presence. He is with me as I write about my teaching journey and understandings. That classroom photo is in front of me as I write this. I am clear that, as I tell my teacher story, I am also giving voice to some of his and honoring the ancestors who inspired him.

During my deep looking, I learned that to explore my intention as a teacher is to connect once more to my uncle and other teaching ancestors and to own the gifts they have transmitted to me. Those gifts are still available. Awareness of my intention helps me to stay connected to my ancestors and to cultivate and share these gifts in my teaching. Thich Nhat Hanh reminds us that our ancestors continue through us. We keep family traditions, stories, skills, and talents alive as we share what we have received with our children and grandchildren. I believe that I am also my teaching ancestors' continuation. When I teach from a place of intention, they are with me in my classroom as I offer their gifts, with mine, to a new generation of learners.

The insight that emerged was that intention, for me, includes two parts, which inter-are, like two sides of a coin. First is my aspiration for who I want to be; second is about my offering to my students. Teaching and learning happen in relationship. For example, a wholesome intention begins with focus on my aspiration about the teacher I want to be, one that is connected to our deep humanity, acknowledging our interbeing: *"I want to make my best offering to all of my students and colleagues from a place of presence and connection."*

As an educator, I also focus intently on supporting my students' growth as learners. Therefore, my mindful intention includes a strong emphasis on my commitment to my students' learning. I promise myself to do my best to help them grow their capacities, which includes planting seeds for lifelong learning. The second part of my intention reflects my responsibility to my students' meaningful learning based on my role. For example, in my work preparing special educators to teach a wide range of students with disabilities: *"I will do my best to prepare special educators who bring both the will and the skills to help all students with disabilities maximize their learning as valued members of inclusive school communities."*

An educator I know who teaches middle school English Language Arts shared this draft of his intention, reflecting his particular field and role:

> *As an 8th grade English Language Arts teacher, I want to connect with each of my students to help them experience the joys and empowerment of reading and writing, and to grow more effective literacy processes and habits as respected members of a community of readers and writers.*

The following intention statement is from a middle school life science educator:

> *As a 7th grade Biology / Ecology teacher, I want to collaborate with all of my students to experience the thrill of discovery through observation and experimentation; the challenge of identifying problems and designing solutions; and the realization of their deep connection to our planet, and to all other beings (i.e., humans, animals, plants and minerals); so that they can contribute to a future of respect and possibility for all.*

I came to learn that a meaningful intention is a broad, student-centered offering. This is learning that matters, at this time, *and* in the future. It cannot be reduced to preparing for certification exams or high scores on mandated assessments. While these outcomes might be real parts of my teaching context, these are specific, measurable outer conditions. Outcomes are important, but only part of what informs my work. When I bring awareness of my inner conditions (intention), this supports my ability to teach from a place of wholeness.

Offering and Outcomes

The energy of my intention can be a source of my teaching as an offering. Over the years since I began my mindfulness practice, I have come to recognize how much of my activity can be tangled up with my expectations for how things will go (i.e., desired outcomes). Too often it seems this can become more about what I want or how it supports my view of myself than about those I am serving. I realized I (my ego) can be strongly attached to outcomes, which in my experience, can seriously limit my ability to make a meaningful offering. I continue to experiment with consciously approaching and sharing my work and service as an offering.

When I am operating from a place of offering, my focus is on myself, before, during, and after my actions. I am the only person whose behavior I can shape. My aim is to stay connected to myself and bring my best effort, before and during an activity. This requires my presence as well as my knowledge and skills. I bring my mindful presence first to my preparation. This helps me to make good decisions about my plans grounded in my professional knowledge and skills. I know and trust when my planning is sufficiently thorough and complete. My planning matches my level of skill and experience for the activity. Over-planning or under-planning indicate that I am anxious and not present. Before implementation, it is most important that I cultivate my ability to be present, so that my actions and interactions will be as skillful as possible. When I am present, I know that I respond more flexibly and draw upon my knowledge and skills, even for unplanned moments. When finished, I first reflect on myself, not the outcome. I am aware of how others participated and responded, but my considerations about others go back to myself. Was my planning appropriate? Is there something I could have done differently that I will consider in the future? Was I present and available during implementation? Were my actions and interactions skillful? What adjustments might I make in the future? If my responses to these questions are mostly positive, I can take satisfaction in meeting my intention to make my best offering. In my experience, when I focus on myself and making my best offering, very often, there are also good outcomes.

Intention and Outcomes

As a lifelong educator, I have spent a lot of time focused on learning outcomes. During my years exploring mindful teaching, I discovered that I could have a different relationship with outcomes when I was in touch with my intention. Rather than being attached to outcomes in ways that raised my anxiety and separated me from my self and my students, I could let them guide my instruction in a more wholesome way. Here is how I currently think about both outcomes and intention based on my experience focused on mindfulness in my work.

Mindful teaching honors both intention and outcomes. Both are necessary and valuable. But intention is different from outcomes. Mindfulness supports my ability to understand, balance and manage these contrasting energies wisely in my daily work and through my career.

Outcomes are an important part of teaching and learning. These offer evidence of how my teaching decisions and actions influence changes in my students' learning. In our current education system, outcomes most often take the form of test scores related to key academic skills and curricula. Other outcome-related teaching elements are curriculum standards, frameworks, and objectives. As an educator, I need to know curricular frameworks, or in my university role, professional competencies and standards, and be able to generate meaningful learning objectives to guide student learning. Standards and objectives allow me to match instruction to students' performance levels as these relate to valued skills and content. Interpreting student learning data can support me to plan in ways that can maximize learning and ensure that my teaching matches student abilities and priorities. These are very much part of my mindful planning and offering.

When I am, additionally, also in touch with my intention, I have more clarity about how to move skillfully toward desired outcomes. I can discern what types of assessments and how much data are needed to support meaningful understandings of my students' learning. With intention, I am still connected to desired outcomes and understand student priorities, and I can trust my capacity to respond with my best offering.

Data, standards, and objectives can be utilized in many ways. What matters is my relationship to these. I know that when outcomes are my singular focus, I become attached to these as my purpose. I tend to be more anxious and therefore more rigid. I can easily become disconnected from myself and my intention and lose touch with some of the best parts of my teaching. My teaching may become rote and skill focused, losing touch with meaning and authentic learning. Too much focus or pressure related to achieving narrowly defined outcomes creates anxiety, which creates loss of presence for teachers and, therefore, for students. This anxiety suffocates my teaching and works against the success of my learners. It carries high costs for both me and my students.

However, if I were to focus only on intention without attention to outcomes, my teaching would also have serious limitations. Disregard for curricular knowledge and skills, meaningful objectives and student progress can create low expectations and limited learning for my students. This could be especially impactful for marginalized groups of learners.

Mindfulness can help me find and maintain my balance. My ongoing partnerships with public schools suggest that our field has over-emphasized narrowly defined outcomes (e.g., test scores) for too long. I wonder how teaching and learning might change if we could find our way back to our intention, as individuals, as teams, as schools. For me, when I am in touch with intention, it helps me to reconnect with the wholeness of my teaching as a noble offering. When I am connected to intention, my teaching can interpret and respond to data skillfully and utilize standards and learning objectives — without compromising the meaning, integrity, and heart of my teaching. My growing awareness of my intention supported the integrity of my teaching, providing a touchstone to invite presence and connection to my inner self, which then often flowed to my students.

There is no conflict between my intention and learning outcomes. My healthy path is one that allows enough space and awareness for both my intention and curricular outcomes to "inter-be" and allow both to guide my teaching. This begins with me creating inner space, being responsible for cultivating my individual intention, regardless of outer conditions.

As an educator, I learned that I need to be aware of and nourish both my inner teacher (intention) and my professional knowledge and skills (curriculum, pedagogy, student characteristics).

Practicing with My Intention

Like mindfulness of feelings, I first cultivate mindfulness of my intention in quiet personal practice. I might spend a few minutes at the end of my morning practice, after I have settled my body and sat with a quiet mind, to briefly reflect on my intention. Who do I aspire to be today as a teacher? What do I want to offer my students today as part of my deep intention to support their learning? I may engage with a resourcing practice and picture a special mentor who recognized and encouraged my capacities (e.g., my uncle, a significant teacher). As I do, I connect with one or a few characteristics they embodied that touched me deeply. I try to see these characteristics in myself, even if they are just seedlings. I feel once more in my body what it was like to be seen, to be encouraged, to receive that person's real attention. As I connect and feel these gifts once more, I strengthen these potentials in my teacher-self. I may reflect on a time when I was particularly skillful in my teaching role; a lesson that flowed, or even a beautiful interaction with a student that lasted only for a few moments. I replay that scenario when I met my intention, feeling once more the energy of deep connection with my inner true teacher-self. I notice the feelings in my body, my solidity, balance, and steady heartbeat. This moment, which may take only a few moments, sets my compass, reconnecting me to my intention for today.

Reflections on Growing Awareness of Intention in My Teaching

With hindsight, I now understand that I was practicing with my intention when I reassessed and made many revisions to my syllabus as I began to "reimagine my university teaching" with mindfulness as described in chapter five. As a college instructor, to examine the big picture, I began with my syllabus and my classroom tone and structures before a new semester began. I looked closely at the learning activities, especially major projects and assessments. I experienced a lot of inner anxiety and perhaps even fear as I began this process. I felt limited by the constraints of the 15-week semester and the amount of professional development necessary for candidates to stay on track for an 18-month program. My daily practice of mindfulness of the body allowed me to begin this effort.

I was already relatively clear on part of my intention for my graduate students who were pursuing a professional path to become special educators. This was based on my broad, long-term view of the teachers I envisioned they could become. I wanted to *"prepare special educators who bring both the will and the skills to help all students with disabilities maximize their learning as valued members of inclusive school communities."* In my field, too often it seems that special educators bring open hearts but are lacking in critical professional knowledge and skills, such as helping students with disabilities maximize their literacy learning. Many students with disabilities receive instruction in separate settings and are denied opportunities to learn with peers who do not have disabilities. In too many cases, they are under-challenged in regard to learning expectations. This part of my intention was already clear and answered the question, *"How do I want to impact my students' learning, now and in the future?"* I saw my teacher preparation role as guiding my candidates to develop key professional competencies, so they would take student learning seriously, and bring teaching skills for inclusive settings for the full range of learners. This intention was much richer, deeper, and broader than preparing my candidates to pass the state teacher certification exam. I was continually referencing this vision of the teachers they could be as I chose priority program experiences and developed meaningful assessments. This helped clarify my work and determine priorities in helping my candidates to develop a solid professional foundation for this complex teacher role.

But my intention, I realized, was also limited. I was very attached to all of my candidates meeting these outcomes at a high level. I believe I took it personally when an individual did not demonstrate capacities that aligned with my vision. I was attached to an outcome; to some degree, their success was about me.

As my mindfulness grew, my intention expanded to focus more on my vision as teacher, and to reframe my work as my best offering. It invited me to ask myself another question related to my intention: *"Who do I aspire to be as a teacher?"* While the first question guided my decisions about content and actions, this question was about *being*, rather than my knowing or doing. Who do I want to *be* in my teaching life? This became part of my intention as well. *"I want to make my best offering as a teacher from a place of presence and connection."* My students were adults who chose to pursue a professional path. Assessment and success were still based on rigorous professional standards. But our human connection in this shared experience mattered, and in my case, needed to be cultivated more.

As I examined my syllabus and some other parts of my practice with this new part of my intention, I realized that functioning as "gatekeeper" could dominate my thinking, especially for candidates who were struggling. This new part of my intention is what guided the changes to my course and syllabus that I described in chapter five. This intention-based examination of broad elements of my teaching and class structures is something

I began to renew each year. My understandings of how best to bring my intention into these big-picture decisions grew and developed over time, as both my mindfulness and teaching experience grew.

Practicing Before and During Challenging Meetings

For meetings with individuals or small groups, I had the advantage of doing some preparation. I would first do some calming practice such as breath or walking meditation before I even began planning for the meeting. From that settled place, I could clarify the purpose of the meeting. Then I reflected on my intention, both who I aspired to be and my responsibilities to students / others, to consider how these informed my participation in the meeting. I might make notes to create a frame for a sequence of a few important points to organize my thinking, especially if I was facilitating. I would actually slow down and visualize myself in the meeting, in the beginning, middle, and end, and hear bits of the skillful language that might emerge. I moved away from over-planning details, but I would take time to let the purpose of the meeting and my intentions inform what I needed to share. My intentions also helped me to let go of saying other things that were not relevant or helpful. Once I was somewhat clear on how my offering in the meeting connected to my intention related to my responsibilities, I focused on the other part of my intention. Who do I aspire to be? How might that aspiration come into this meeting? For me this is very simple. It is about my presence. I made time, if possible, shortly before the meeting, to practice in order to calm my body and ground myself with breathing. I began the meeting slowly, taking a few breaths. I began with words of kindness and some positive points about the person or their work. I tried to let the meeting unfold without rushing, but stayed connected to the purpose and key points. These were big changes for me, especially slowing down and letting go of some control.

The end of semester conference with my graduate student Anna, which I described in chapter five, is an example of a time that I was successful in bringing both mindfulness and intention to our meeting. Recall that we were near the end of the semester and that Anna's performance in her coursework, including her planning and reading instruction for tutoring, was not meeting criteria based on professional standards to successfully complete the course. Part of my intention (*Prepare special educators who bring both the will and the skills to help all students with disabilities maximize their learning*) included the requirement that students demonstrate key professional competencies for individualized reading instruction. This intention was not only about my candidates, but the children with disabilities they would teach in the future, possibly for decades. My decisions impacted the hundreds of school-age students they would touch. I needed to inform Anna that she would not be receiving a passing grade, which meant she would not go further in the graduate program. To assign a passing grade would not be aligned with my intention. I wanted to help her understand how her performance related to the criteria and the grade.

The other part of my intention (*To make my best offering as a teacher from a place of presence and connection*) was also part of my preparation. I wanted to be present and connected to Anna during this conversation. I knew this would be painful news for her. It made me very anxious to deliver this bad news and, in the past, I may have disconnected as a person while sharing the news. In the past, I might have focused on telling the student multiple ways their work fell short of the criteria, referencing multiple examples from my documentation. It would not have been a conversation. This time, I reflected on who I wanted to be in this meeting to, if possible, support Anna's experience in receiving and understanding this news. I did extra meditation before class. I took a short time to settle myself after the three-hour class to regain presence before we began talking. I made that space, saying to her something like, "I need about 5 minutes. Take a little break for yourself and then we will talk." (This was to settle my body and calm my emotions.) Anna did not pass this course and field experience. But I was able to meet my intention to give fair and accurate feedback while I remained present and connected to her. She left our meeting with more understanding and clarity about when she is present and effective in her teaching and could assess her teaching more accurately. I also believe she left feeling valued and supported as a person.

Looking back once more at my unsuccessful consultation with young Misha (chapter three), I did begin with practices grounded in mindfulness of the body, both in daily practice and before our time began. However, I was not operating from a wholesome intention. I had not reflected on my intention before our experience. I now realize that I came with an agenda, and it was self-serving. I was hoping to recreate the wonderful experience I had with Damien — and get videotape of my imagined shared literacy experience to use in my teaching. I was attached to an outcome. And that outcome had nothing to do with a meaningful offering for Misha during our shared time. I also had not reflected on who or how I wanted to be in our experience in my preparation. Even my planning had been primarily task- and materials-focused, based on the outcome I desired.

When I had another chance to explore literacy learning with a student with developmental disabilities (Keira, chapter four), I approached things differently, and with much more humility. Recall that my work was to assess Keira's literacy capacities, not to provide instruction. I went in curious, as I had been with Damien. I was not sure what might unfold and had no specific outcome in mind. My intention was to begin from a place of solidity and stay present throughout our time. I prepared more diligently in my daily practice. I was more aware in my practice before we began. I was also, of course, prepared to offer and facilitate some authentic literacy activities to learn about her abilities, learning priorities, and possible tools and practices. With mindfulness, I stayed connected to this as an offering that might support Keira's educational opportunities. I maintained a slower, steady pace and was calm and inviting in my facilitation. I had a broader intention to "*learn about conditions that might support Keira's continued engagement and growth as a reader and writer for learning and enjoyment.*" While my failed experiment with Misha was painful, it highlighted my need to clarify and bring intention as a critical element of mindful teaching. My experience with Keira affirmed this direction in my work. And, like my work with Damien, it "felt" right.

Practicing in the Moment

This is very challenging. I practice to do my best to maintain my focus on myself and my inner experience during the flow of my teaching work. To create conditions that were supportive, I would arrive early for classes and organize my materials and the space so that I would not be rushed. Sometimes I would do a few minutes of personal practice. This might include mindful walking to the classroom as I was arriving. I might take a few minutes for a stillness practice once things were set up.

One time when my growing mindfulness practice supported my ability to respond and not react in the moment was during a large department meeting. I was presenting a proposal for a new master's program to prepare special educators for middle and high school learners. There was a desperate need for secondary special educators in our region and state. New program proposals required faculty and committee support at many levels, beginning with the department. After my presentation offered an overview, faculty members were invited to ask questions. Several individuals made affirming comments about addressing this need; others asked for clarification about meaningful issues related to resources and implementation. The vibe was overall supportive and positive. Then a colleague who was often extremely negative about my work and the special education graduate programs raised his hand. His "question" was essentially a critical attack on both our current programs and this proposal. The room fell silent. The flow of interaction was shut down instantly. The atmosphere shifted to a palpable sense of uncertainty about what might come next. I felt all eyes on me. In the past, I would have likely taken a strong defensive stance; my tone could have been antagonistic. This time, however, I did not react. There was a brief pause. I recall feeling hurt, rather than angry with this person. I felt a heaviness in my body, my heart sank a bit in sadness. Then, I calmly replied in a quiet voice, "This is a proposal. Of course, everyone gets to vote." My tone was vulnerable, honoring the hurt. The collective energy in the room seemed to relax immediately. We moved on. Following the meeting, I replayed that brief interaction in my mind, thinking about how this moment captured the person I want to be in all of my interactions — stable, calm, respectful. I recognized that even with my strong patterns of verbal reactivity that I had consolidated for many, many years, change was possible. In that moment, I was able to respond to a public personal attack while maintaining my presence and my connection to my true self. I had met my intention. The clearest sign that I had remained present was my awareness of my vulnerability.

Over time, my insight about intention revealed many layers for deep looking and for my practice. As I developed awareness of my intention in my personal practice, I began to sometimes feel its presence lightly accompanying me through my daily teaching work. It seems this is the element that supports my teaching from the heart to make my work a beautiful offering. The power of my teaching path flows from the inside. It was mindfulness that helped me to awaken to this inner energy of my aspiration and my teaching ancestors. It benefits me to nurture, explore, and sustain my connection to it.

The following section will share ways I began to share mindfulness practices with my graduate student candidates, including invitations for their own explorations in their teaching. I also discuss examples from their reflections on their own experiences.

Part Four

Mindful Teaching: Learning with and from Teacher Candidates

After several years of deep exploration and changes to my own teaching, I began (slowly) to introduce my graduate students to some mindfulness practices. Chapters ten and eleven describe how this grew into mindful teaching experiments for my candidates over the years that followed; experiments that also supported and nourished my practice.

NOTE: All *italicized candidate quotes* in Part Four are from individuals who granted permission to share verbatim from their written reflections during graduate studies or from conversations with me about their mindful teaching explorations.

Chapter 10

Guiding Others: Helping Pre-Service Teachers Explore Mindful Teaching

For several years I focused my experiments only on my own teaching practice. I did not talk with my candidates about mindfulness or my shifting practice. My awareness of the positive impact on my teaching offering grew. I recognized how mindfulness helped me to bring a more settled and steady energy to the classroom, how I was developing increased skill in communication in difficult situations, and how I experienced increasing clarity in my planning. Anxiety, which was sometimes misperceived as passion or enthusiasm, was no longer driving my teaching. I recognized that mindfulness practice was unlocking my teacher potential far more than anything else I had learned or experienced as an educator. I felt increasingly drawn to sharing some tools for mindfulness with my candidates, who were preparing to begin their careers as educators in a very complex role. My experience suggested this was one of the most important and empowering experiences I could offer to support these beginning educators to make their best offering, now and in the future.

I began slowly. Mindfulness was not yet "mainstream." I had some concerns about resistance to what might be perceived as me imposing some non-Western spiritual beliefs at a public university. I was intentional about sharing practices in completely secular ways. I recall the first time I shared practices explicitly with my graduate class. In the first few classes, I talked more openly about the idea of mindfulness and staying present and read some of my own log entries. I read significant parts of my Damien journal entry and another reflection aloud.

Then I guided a breath meditation for about 5 minutes. We talked about how it felt. I invited them to say (by secret ballot) if they wanted to do this before every class. Everyone said yes (or yes, please). After that we began taking a few minutes before grad class to close our eyes and breathe intentionally. The first year, a few weeks in, some people were rustling papers and trying to calculate their tutees' assessments during our quiet breathing time. I felt irritated. I did not know what to do. I wondered if we should give up. The next class I talked openly about this. I said, "We talked about this the first week and you agreed to experiment with opening with this practice. It's okay if you choose not to engage with this and do the breathing. But please be still and respect the quiet for those of us who want to practice. I do want to and need to before every class. I will be more available to you if you support me in this way." It was still from then on.

Each subsequent semester I expanded the sharing to eventually include more explicit examples of how I was trying to apply mindfulness in my teaching. I became clearer on my priorities for sharing practice with these beginning educators. First, I wanted their introduction to mindfulness to be grounded in their experience with *practice*. I wanted to invite them to be open to exploring mindfulness in *multiple aspects of their teaching* work as I had (e.g., to notice and tend emotional stress, to plan with awareness, to be aware of moments of connection and flow, to notice when they disconnect from presence, to notice and reset themselves, to stay with their discomfort and try to respond with intention in the moment). Also, I wanted to create conditions to support *their ownership of their individual practice through ongoing reflection and experimentation*, especially in their teaching. In this chapter I will share how I integrated mindful teaching increasingly through the years, and some examples of candidates' experiences of this, based on their own writing about their experiences.

Nurturing Mindful Teaching

Each fall I taught a six-credit block on Reading for Special Educators. It included a reading clinic experience. Each graduate student was assigned to an elementary student for the semester; a first or second grader who needed extra help in learning to read. We met twice a week. The first hour was one-on-one tutoring. I was present to observe and support. The next 2 hours were devoted to our graduate class on reading intervention.

One of the assignments that shifted as we began exploring mindfulness was the "Teaching Log." This used to be focused on the young student. It became one of the primary tools we used to prompt and support "mindful" teaching. This log supported graduate student tutors to be present to and to reflect on their own experience. Some semesters, we would take 10 minutes after tutoring at the beginning of grad class for stillness so people could write privately in their journals (which I never collected or read).

As we began to focus on mindful teaching, graduate students were asked to develop two or three short "reflection pieces" a semester (ungraded). These were submitted along with self-assessment of sample videotaped lessons. Reflections sometimes referenced patterns they noticed in their private journals to write about their changing perceptions and experiences.

I shared the following description with students to guide the Mindful Teaching reflections.

<u>Mindful Teaching Reflections</u> (Monitoring Authentic or Mindful Teaching)

Beginning in October, provide written thoughts (2–3 pages) as scheduled. These should focus on your insights and analysis of your teaching experience as it relates to this context. This is not a summary / description of sessions or of your student's participation, but examples of what you are noticing about your self in the context of teaching: how you are experimenting with staying mindful / present in your teaching. For example, you might discuss what you are noticing about any physical sensations that arise in your body or about emotions / feelings you notice, especially during moments of difficulty. You might share what you notice about your response patterns, how you are monitoring and managing your "self" and your anxiety in relation to your decision making (especially "in the moment"), and your efforts to stay present and trust your self and your growing experience even during challenging moments. You might discuss how you are identifying and working with your "thought" patterns as these relate to positive and challenging moments before, during and after teaching interactions. Ground your thinking in actual examples from your experience (including interactions with your student or planning experiences). You might also discuss examples when you recognize that you fulfilled your intention, hunches about what triggers your reactivity, possible experiments you are considering to work with patterns you have identified, or how your experiments are playing out. Mostly this log is a tool to be intentional about practicing being present and mindful to your teaching experience.

The content of your reflections will not be graded. This is an opportunity for me to respond to and support your experimentation with "mindful" teaching — staying present and connected to self, and trusting yourself as you plan, teach and interpret your ongoing experience. It will also help me to reflect on how to better support teachers' learning about mindful teaching.

The first few times I received mindful teaching reflections, I was surprised by and excited about many of the comments. Nearly all members had something that was appropriate and related to their experience and mindfulness. I responded to each individually and privately on Blackboard, our online course management system. It was encouraging to read and respond. These interactions allowed me to feel connected to my students in new and meaningful ways. Below I offer excerpts from some reflections, including some of my responses.

One candidate wrote about how her anxiety can quickly escalate during tutoring. She described how she experienced "rising fear" if things went a little differently than she had planned or when the student responded differently than she anticipated. If such moments occurred while I was in the space floating and observing, this was even more intense. She wrote that she tried to hold her intention to stay present, trusting that her best responses came when she was calm. She noted that in such moments of presence, she was unaware of what else was going on in the room, with other tutors or whether I was there to observe. She went on to say that when she felt anxious, she questioned herself and felt unsure about everything. She reported that in these moments she sometimes remembered to breathe or recalled some of my suggestions or excerpts of encouraging readings that were shared. She had noticed how her energy did seem to affect her student, both when she was present and settled, and when she felt anxious and flustered. She said that the continuous reminders in our graduate class to do our best to try to be present had helped her not only during tutoring, but also at other times throughout her day.

This student went on to share an anecdote about arriving for tutoring one day and realizing she had not printed her lesson plan. Each tutoring session was an hour-long lesson with five different "sub-lessons." She initially panicked, knowing she would not have the written plan to reference. However, she realized the plan was fresh in her head, then "took a breath," and told herself that nothing terrible was going to happen. She recalled me encouraging them to just "do their best" in an unexpected teaching moment, joking that "no one is going to die" if they could not always find the most precise or beneficial teaching language. She went on to say that the lesson flowed beautifully, better than expected. In fact, she actually felt focused and present, and both she and the student were coordinated and comfortable throughout. She was aware that her teaching was specific and clear, and well matched to the student's goals. The student concluded by saying this turned out to be a very good experience.

The following was my response to the candidate's reflection (reproduced verbatim, save for minor edits):

I love the example of forgetting to print the lesson plan. I have had this kind of experience. The anxiety came up – no surprise there – but you did not let it take over. You recognized it, put it in its place and focused on your self in that moment – and surprise, you did it. The evidence that you got your self present again in this lesson is how well it went (even better than expected!). Remember that feeling. Trust it. Notice and remember the kind of things that help you (breathing, quotes from readings, self-talk, "no one is going to die..."). These are also good examples of your awareness – and ability – to use your "resources" such as these tools to get yourself back to the present. Keep in mind that I intended these as suggestions for you to consider – if relevant for your experiments and helpful to you! Please don't think of them as "what you were told to do."

Another student wrote that the anxiety before each tutoring lesson never went away, although she was always well prepared. She described constant worry that her student might not "get it" or (even more commonly) wouldn't open up and talk during the lesson. She told me that she always wanted her lessons to be perfect, and spent a lot of time analyzing her decisions, even during the lesson. She said she often got pulled out of presence even while teaching, questioning her plan for the next activity. She knew she was often caught in worries about the future, and not fully present for the activity she was guiding. She expressed a desire to be "looser" and more relaxed with her student during her lessons. She went on to express her concerns about his shyness and limited interactions, and reported focusing a lot of her energy on trying to get him to be looser and let go. But, she said, they always got the work done. She talked about how she got her student to smile a few times in the previous week. She reported on one occasion when he did open up and shared more extensively about losing a tooth and playing with his brother over the weekend. She enjoyed this and noted that he initiated this sharing. She closed by saying each day she worried about whether her student liked her, and why he was so much less talkative than other students who were with tutors in their shared classroom space.

My response:

Such mindful thinking here. Wonderful that you are aware of your desire for lessons to be "perfect" and to get the "task" done. This theme resonates through several comments and connects to some of your observations. Really great that you notice that your mind is sometimes ahead of the lesson – jumping into the future like the discussion questions or possible revisions. The idea of trying to be more "natural" might be a worthy experiment. What would it take for you to try out being more natural and stay with him? Also, good that you notice that you are always "trying" to "get him to open up." Ask yourself: How is that working? You might just experiment with "not trying" for a couple of lessons and see what happens. Do you wonder why you want him to be different? Great stuff here. Lots of opportunities for experimentation with your patterns / habit energies as you teach in this context. Like you, I really trust the time he got talking because he initiated it. Keep paying attention to the moments / conditions when he can / does initiate.

Introducing a Foundation for Mindful Teaching

In the semesters that followed, I became braver and slowly increased my explicit sharing of mindfulness practices at the beginning of the semester. I also explored ways to help candidates experiment with the practice in their teaching, during and beyond this first semester of field work. Eventually, in the last few years, I dedicated a full class (second meeting of the semester) to facilitating experiences with mindfulness practices. We followed this up with a week of "homework" to experiment with a personal daily mindfulness practice and to write briefly about it each day. Eventually, I began meeting with all tutors before each tutoring session for 5 minutes of group practice with guided meditation. Candidates continued to submit two longer reflections on their mindful teaching each semester as part of their self-evaluation in their literacy instruction experience. My colleague Amanda and I alternated semesters teaching the final internship seminar. With her support, I revised the weekly writing prompts for the seminar to add a brief reflection on examples of how they were integrating mindfulness into their experience in the special educator role in their internship setting. For nearly all candidates, the internship occurred a full year after the literacy block where they were introduced to mindful teaching. During the second semester, I had no contact with candidates, and they had no explicit instruction or support focused on mindfulness. I share more about each of these experiments, and some student responses, in the pages that follow.

Before we unpack these efforts, however, it is important to note that I spent very little time in the courses and field placements teaching candidates *about* mindfulness. Both the six-credit literacy course (with tutoring) and the final full-time internship in the special educator role had many professional requirements to learn and apply, with respect to assessment, curriculum, and pedagogy. My efforts to introduce mindfulness focused on providing an early experience at the beginning of the first semester, and encouragement with feedback to continue their practice. In my final semester teaching the literacy block to first-semester graduate candidates, the following represented the sum total of experiences focused on mindfulness in this introductory experience in the first semester of this graduate program:

- Week 1, Class 2: We discussed considerations for a mindful approach to organizing conditions in their life and schedule to best support themselves holistically for this challenging first semester of graduate school. This included a focus on self-care routines with attention to sleep, healthy eating, and exercise. I also invited reflection on conditions that increase or decrease stress. I suggested that, during this challenging time in their lives with work and graduate studies, they make choices to minimize activities and time with people who drained them or increased their anxiety. I offered permission and language to support boundaries to care for their needs. I asked them to privately identify conditions that nourished them, and suggested more, encouraging them to be sure to build in times daily to water their positive seeds.
- We then spent 2.5 hours experiencing facilitated mindfulness practices, with my guidance and free apps. First, I introduced and facilitated some practices, including guided breath meditation, silent sitting meditation with bell for 5 minutes, walking meditation, and eating meditation. We also listened to and practiced with guided meditations from several free apps (breath meditation, body scan, calming anxiety). There was time for processing and sharing individual experiences after each.

- Week 1, homework before next class (no tutoring yet): Candidates read three short articles about the benefits of mindfulness, viewed a brief video clip, and wrote a brief response to this set of resources. Candidates were instructed to implement daily 10-minute personal mindfulness practice (at least five every seven days) using apps for guided meditations if desired. (We had tried apps out together in class.) Candidates were instructed to post a short reflection EACH day on Blackboard (the online course management system) about each day's experience. I would write back to each candidate at the end of the week (not daily) to make space for their own experiments and adjustments.
- Class 3. Brief full group processing about their mindfulness experiments, highlighting some of the observations they had shared in their writing (10–15 minutes). I encouraged them to continue their experiments to support themselves in their teaching and other experiences. Most of class focused on literacy-related material such as planning assessments for tutees.
- Tutoring began Week 3. Before each tutoring session (twice a week), we met briefly as a group. I facilitated a 5-minute stillness meditation, then tutors went to pick up their students for tutoring.
- Twice a semester, candidates submitted a two-page reflection on their mindful teaching efforts, including examples from their tutoring (or sometimes other teaching, such as subbing). This was a piece they submitted with a larger self-evaluation that included a videotaped lesson analysis and lesson plans. The mindful teaching reflection was not graded. I wrote back to each individual, highlighting examples of mindfulness and encouraging / suggesting other possibilities.

This literacy course was a six-credit experience that met twice a week. There were about 28 class meetings and about 20 tutoring sessions for the semester. As noted, we spent little time learning *about* or discussing mindfulness during the weekly graduate classes. However, I remained very intentional about my personal mindfulness practice and integrating this into my teaching and interactions with candidates. When I met with candidates individually for conferences or problem solving, I would inquire about and encourage ways to integrate their mindfulness practice within their planning and teaching process for this situation, but much of this time was focused on understandings and teacher decision making for literacy. The structured, bi-weekly field experience (supervised by me) presented ongoing motivation and opportunities for candidates to explore mindfulness as an integral part of their growing teaching practice. This experience included a lot of challenging new professional learning (e.g., literacy process, data-based instruction, individualized planning, and interventions for a reader who is making limited progress). The fact that tutors had only one student for this focused experiment offered supportive conditions for beginning explorations of mindful teaching. A year later, in their third and final semester, candidates were in a far more complex role, with many more students and broader responsibilities during their full-time internship semester as a special educator.

In addition to her comments about her efforts to stay mindful during tutoring, another candidate broadened the lens to question the role of mindfulness in the rest of her life. She reflected on having too many responsibilities, and how her weekly preparation for graduate classes and teaching consumed much of her time. She was aware that she worked hard in her planning for her lessons and tried her best to be present during her teaching, but she wondered about the rest of her life. Since beginning grad school, she had felt that there was so much to do that she had little time to pause or reflect. She reported that she was constantly reading and planning and writing for multiple classes, and that weekends were filled with other obligations. She reflected on her awareness that she viewed so much in her life as temporary. She went on to say how she thought ahead to how, when grad school ended, she could pursue the teaching position she wanted, and have more time with her partner and, perhaps in the future, her children. She felt like so many parts of her vision were on hold while she finished things — in this case, grad school. She was constantly distracted in her life outside of school by the work that was waiting. She wondered how she might achieve more balance.

My response:

Great questions. I really appreciate your honesty — and that you are broadening the lens to ask about how present you are in all of the spheres of your life. Of course, this IS the real question. And you are wise to ask about finding balance — that is the constant goal and challenge. Most people are not even aware they are not in balance or that this might be possible. This alone says you are being present to your experience. I wonder how much time you are spending on prep for classes and tutoring. You are very thorough and well prepared. How long does this take? Is it more than is necessary for you?

I appreciate your comments about how it is hard to stop and notice our experience when we are so busy doing so many things that need to be done. It is true that too much doing gets in the way of presence and awareness — these are grounded in "being" — which requires that we stop from time to time — stop even our thinking. My present life also feels too busy and includes too many responsibilities. For me, it is making myself take time every day — even a few minutes — to intentionally breathe and be and to stop thinking. This includes time early in the morning before my day begins, and time whenever I remember between activities. Sometimes it is only 2 or 3 minutes. But it helps me get grounded and try to be more present with myself before I begin the next task. Another thing for me is to try to do one thing at a time; to push away thoughts about the things that are waiting. This includes trying to give my full attention to family and friends when I am with them — not just "responsibilities." It is not easy. Our human brains are programmed to do otherwise. But I am mostly trying to stay friends with my mind even if I don't always follow where it wants to go. Your observations about looking at things as "temporary" are interesting. Keep exploring this. Of course, everything is temporary — our jobs, our relationships, our lives. What else are you noticing when you say this? Does this thinking about things as only temporary help or hinder you from being present in the current experience? That is, does it mostly focus you more on this experience or often pull you into future thoughts about "life after this experience" (such as life after grad school)? Your writing reflects a lot of mindfulness as you struggle with these questions. Presence can be uncomfortable — that's why we humans always are trying to distract ourselves!

The following reflection was submitted by a candidate at the end of her first semester.

I never thought that in my graduate level class I would be learning how to be mindful while teaching. I have been working with children since I turned 13 and I cannot help but wonder, why has no one told me about this before? I have learned that every minute, I have a choice to be present and in the moment.

While working with Nicholas, I find myself still wavering from being 100% in the moment, to not being mindful at all. When I first started working with Nicholas, it was easier to be mindful. He did not display any challenging behaviors and was eager to learn and read. I felt like I was in the moment while assessing Nicholas' present levels of performance. I enjoyed seeing him thrive and was excited to teach to address his individual needs.

A time where I am always mindful is when Nicholas and I first sit down and talk before we start working. I thoroughly enjoy having authentic conversations with Nicholas about his hopes, dreams, and more importantly, his current life. I've learned so much about him that affects my book choice and my conversation topics that I would not have known if I was not mindful while he eats his snack. I believe Nicholas can sense that I am fully present and listening. I do not think he would share as much with me otherwise.

Lately, Nicholas has presented some challenging behaviors that I need to learn to be mindful about, trying to avoid being reactive. In the past two lessons, Nicholas has become resistant to reading and working. I tell him what the plan is, and he says, "I don't wanna." He has been seeking control any way possible, including asking me to turn the pages of the book for him. This is not the behavior I am familiar with from him and was unprepared this week to handle it mindfully. At one point I got very annoyed, and I could hear my negative tone and feel it in my face. It was a wakeup call; I was not being mindful. I took a deep breath and made the decision to be mindful. I told Nicholas what the plan was again, and laid out the supplies so he would have a visual. I gave him choices where I could and let him help where he could (putting paperclips back on the phonics cards when we finished). It seemed to work better, but I need to change the way I have been teaching. I have a tendency to enjoy being in control. It is hard to let Nicholas do things like putting paperclips on cards when I know I can complete the task quicker. I need to be mindful of Nicholas's personality and mindful of my own.

Next week I am going to experiment with having a visual schedule with Nicholas. I need to set clearer expectations for Nicholas so he knows what is expected and we are not struggling over power. I need to be mindful that I am the teacher and I get to choose the type of teacher I want to be. I can be caring and helpful while still being firm.

My Response:

Your reflections offer such wonderful understandings of mindfulness and your commitment to taking responsibility to be a mindful teacher, especially when things are not easy. This mindful approach is informing your intentional decisions about how to support Nicholas' participation and deal with behavioral challenges both proactively and in the moment. Mostly, what I hear is, "Who do I want to be as Nicholas' teacher?" I look forward to hearing more.

While I had some initial concern about how candidates might respond to my sharing of meditation practices, there was no resistance. A very small number (maybe two over the years) were not able to write about their experience, and their reflections continued to focus on their students. I always shared in a secular way and framed the offering as a potential support to care for themselves and their learning. After a couple of semesters, I made more explicit connections to potential teaching and learning benefits with their students. As I offered more experiences and support in the later years, engagement and interest grew. Having the tutoring experience before each graduate class offered a context for their teaching experiments each week. It was also clear that their participation and writing related to mindful teaching were completely ungraded.

Prompting and Supporting Mindfulness During Full-Time Internship

During their third and final graduate semester, candidates were placed in public schools for a full-time, 10-week internship in the special education role. This was one year after the semester in which candidates were introduced to mindfulness. They worked within a team of general and special educators, under the mentorship of an experienced special educator. Full-time college faculty (myself or my colleague Amanda) supervised candidates closely throughout the placement, visiting at least every 2 weeks. One of us also taught the weekly seminar course that accompanied the internship each semester. During face-to-face seminar meetings, we supported various candidate experiences and competencies. These included growing their capacities to work with paraprofessionals; planning and implementing an action research project in their placement and preparing to share findings at a professional conference; and preparing for their job search and interviews. Many online seminar activities required candidates to post and share samples of professional work from their varied placements with one another and seminar faculty (e.g., literacy assessment summaries, lesson plans, behavior intervention assessments, and collaborative planning products). Later, these online activities also included weekly writing prompts that invited candidates to reflect on their inner experience and to explore these with mindfulness. No additional time was devoted to teaching about mindfulness or practicing with candidates during this semester. Each week, candidates shared their postings with a peer and wrote brief responses to each other about their work and reflections. Faculty viewed all postings each week.

The following are examples of seminar writing prompts intended to support mindfulness through reflection on one's inner experience, as it intersects with the special educator role and decision making in this real teaching context.

<u>Weekly Seminar Prompts for Interns Related to Mindfulness (Choose one per week)</u>

Briefly describe your placement's context — type of school; special education service model; grades, ages, and other characteristics of students; general education, paraprofessionals, and other teammates (less than ½ p.).

What impressions / responses have emerged for you so far about the special educator's role, schedule, responsibilities, pace ... other? Be honest. How is it similar to what you expected? What surprised you? How does it seem similar to or different from other teacher roles you have experienced (e.g., general educator)? What are you experiencing now? What kinds of anxieties or patterns will you need to monitor and work with to stay mindful and make your best decisions?

Discuss one example of an ongoing role or responsibility in your placement where you experience confidence and feel you are able to be more present and effective.

Discuss one example of a challenging situation that can create worry / stress / anxiety for you. Describe your observations about your thoughts and body sensations, feelings, and reactive responses you have noticed you take to escape or control the anxiety, and your vision for what it would be like if you stayed present (desired response). Include a few ideas for how you are working with this (or might experiment) to manage your stress and stay more present (even if it still feels uncomfortable — the goal is to stay, not to "feel better"). Note any observations about student / adult responses related to your effort to work with mindfulness.

Describe an instructional experience from the past week. Discuss evidence of when you were mindful and present and how that went for you — and students. Describe what you might do in the future based on effective features. Note one or more moments when you lost your mindfulness and describe YOUR experience. What might you do differently in the future in this same kind of lesson to manage your stress and stay more present?

Describe an instructional role / responsibility where you have grown and are gaining confidence. Give examples of evidence of your changes; provide an update on a situation where you are intentionally working with your mindfulness (with students or colleagues).

Describe your experience facilitating the team meeting to share patterns / outcomes of the focus student's Functional

Behavior Assessment to begin team planning of a Behavior Intervention Plan. Who attended? Describe everything YOU did to prepare and facilitate the process. Include your experience before and during, and how you worked with mindfulness practices to maximize the effectiveness and integrity of the process. Note your role for initiating and monitoring implementation of the Behavior Intervention Plan.

This internship was a far more complex role than the initial experience with one-on-one tutoring. Candidates were now taking on many parts of the special educator role for a full-time 10-week experience within a public-school team. Teams included another special educator, one or more general educators, and one or more paraprofessionals (teacher assistants). The conditions for the unknown and anxiety were real. The prompts for their seminar reflections were an effort to remind them of their mindfulness practice as a resource during this intense and challenging experience. Here are some of the kinds of responses from candidate postings in their weekly seminar reflections.

One candidate wrote about how the English Language Arts block was a very difficult time for her to stay present. The context was a co-teaching situation in a general education class with both another special educator and the classroom teacher (who were new partners). There was sometimes tension between the teaching partners, which she was aware raised her anxiety. She also realized part of her stress was because she was not informed of the curriculum for each lesson ahead of time. She noticed that at times during that session, she found her mind thinking ahead to the next group she would teach in a resource room, or about anticipated stressors when the school day ended. But she went on to share how she planned to experiment with bringing mindfulness to this situation. She had begun practicing a short breathing exercise at the end of lunch each day, prior to that class, to reset. She had also talked with her mentor special education teacher (one of the co-teachers) to get more detailed plans for the week for that class so that she could be clearer on and better prepared for her teaching role during that time. She expected this might alleviate some of her stress and uncertainty.

This intern provided a very honest reflection about how her lack of confidence with the team's English Language Arts time challenged her ability to be present, as she found her distracted mind constantly pulled into the future and other worries. She was also aware of how perceived tensions between her co-teaching teammates raised her stress. Her mindful response reflected that she recognized that work with her self was the only currently available remedy to these. It is noteworthy that the response she chose includes both working with her mindfulness to become steady and present before this challenging lesson begins each day, *and* strengthening her ability to be more effective with the curriculum and instruction during this time. By taking initiative to request more information about the curriculum and general education teachers' lesson plans a week early, she was better prepared, more confident, and reduced some of this source of anxiety.

Another candidate wrote about how she was aware of her growing ability to be more present in communicating with her professional teammates, both special education and general educators. She noted that while she had previously been somewhat passive, worried about others' responses, she was increasingly becoming able to share some of her perspectives and ideas within the team. She went on to say that she felt quite challenged about communicating with teaching assistants as she became responsible for planning their work with some students, as well as offering feedback and support. While she understood and accepted that this is one of the responsibilities of a special educator, she felt that, as intern, she did not have the authority to tell them what to do. She admitted that she had had no negative responses from the teaching assistants about her guidance, but her discomfort was still strong. She conveyed how she was practicing to be mindful of her tone and how she talked to the teaching assistants so that she did not sound peremptory or condescending.

This reflection included awareness of how mindfulness was supporting this individual's growth to own and share her professional knowledge. It also highlighted a common challenging experience: as an intern, and as a young professional, it can be stressful to manage and guide other adults, such as paraprofessional team members. These teaching assistants often have years of experience in their job and may be much older than the intern or beginning teachers. This intern was aware of her internal experience and anxiety about this part of her role, but was mindful to pay attention to herself and her speech within these interactions. She noticed that her perception about what TAs think about her providing direction may not be true. She also acknowledged her professional responsibility to plan for teaching assistants. She experimented with mindful, "gentle" speech with paraprofessional team members when guiding them or delegating responsibilities for their work with students.

Another candidate wrote about how mindfulness is supporting her efforts to share more in team meetings, even when she anticipates that her sharing may not be well received. She was aware that, in the past, she would tend to avoid sharing dissenting opinions or perspectives in order to avoid conflict. She was pleased to report that she was beginning to find her voice at times, even among more experienced colleagues. She described focusing extensively on how to share her thinking respectfully. She went on to share a specific example of co-planning for a math lesson that included students with and without disabilities. This intern advocated for allowing the students to use some of their tools (fraction strips), since the lesson was focused on understanding and applying the concepts. She knew some of the students with disabilities could not carry out the application activity successfully without this tool. Ultimately, the general education partner agreed to try it for one lesson, and then reported back to the intern that she felt the activity was much more successful for all of the students. The intern concluded by writing that she was aware that if she had not spoken up, a number of her students (who have disabilities) would have been frustrated and experienced no learning.

This candidate expressed how mindfulness of her professional responsibility (to help all learners, including those with disabilities, to engage and learn) was interacting with her tendency to "defer to teammates" rather than share her ideas. Mindfulness allowed her to choose to practice with sharing her ideas with colleagues respectfully, and to advocate for learners, even when others disagree.

My experience supporting my pre-service teachers in their ongoing experiments with mindful teaching enriched my practice and offered many insights. Even in the very first semester, most wrote about significant shifts to focus on their inner experience, becoming a witness to body sensations, feelings and thoughts that came up, signaling anxiety. Many of their examples document a growing acceptance and tolerance of uncomfortable body sensations and thoughts. Some were able to describe how, when they noticed these arising, they chose actions to settle themselves (e.g., breathing, self-talk), allowing them to respond with awareness of their teaching intentions, rather than react to escape the anxiety. Many examples in their writing documented how their growing mindfulness supported their decision making in challenging moments, as well as post instruction reflections and planning adjustments. Candidates were invited to write about instances in which they were able to bring mindfulness to their teaching. The examples are not necessarily reflective of consistent teaching behaviors, but more likely reflect their "best" moments. Nevertheless, the examples document a growing understanding of mindful teaching grounded in intention, and the powerful possibilities it represents for teachers and learners.

My students' mindful teaching explorations provided encouragement each semester. It was deeply satisfying to read logs about mindful teaching from interns, especially in the later years when I had offered more direct preparation in mindfulness. Though there was a period of nine months with no further support or instruction with mindfulness between the literacy block and the internship, many continued to apply what they had learned. Some of the internship reflections document times when they responded mindfully in far more complex full-time teaching roles with groups of students, a range of curricula, and new adult teammates.

Chapter Eleven offers more exploration and interpretation of mindful teaching examples as reported by candidates. The majority of these examples were shared during their final semester (full-time internship), and for a few, when they were in their first teaching positions.

Chapter 11

Making Meaning: Candidate Reflections and Insights

In Part Three (chapters seven through nine), I discussed significant insights from my mindful teaching explorations: professional knowledge, skills, and dispositions; awareness of and response to inner experiences; and intention as vision and compass. These three insights emerged over time as I reflected on my personal mindfulness experiments in my teaching. I had not yet identified these insights during my teaching years, and therefore had not explicitly shared these with candidates as central elements of mindful teaching. Toward the end of my writing process, after these insights became clear to me, I revisited comments I had collected from my teacher candidates in my final three years of teaching. This was the period during which I had offered the most support for personal practice and mindful teaching to candidates (i.e., during the initial literacy block in their first year of graduate studies). I was curious to find out if their self-reported experiences with mindful teaching would relate to any of the three insights that grew out of my own explorations. I discovered that multiple examples shared by candidates about their mindful teaching related to one or more of the insights that were important to my experience.

The source of the candidate experiences I share in this section came from re-reading the written reflections submitted during their graduate work (i.e., the literacy block and many from the internship semester). Some comments also come from interviews with a few candidates who remained engaged with their mindful teaching practice in their beginning teacher positions and stayed connected with me.

The reflections shared by candidates during their full-time internship were based on planning and teaching activities with a wide range of learners, in various public elementary schools. During the internship, nearly all candidates were in different schools and had little or no access to classmates from this graduate program who had shared an initial experience with mindful teaching in prior semesters.

In the pages that follow I will share examples of some of the mindful teaching experiences offered by candidates that align with the insights that emerged for me.

Professional Knowledge, Skills, and Dispositions Matter

One candidate wrote about noticing that she was questioning herself about her plans for academic lessons with students she served who have disabilities. She recalled that in prior field experiences, she always felt confident in challenging her students appropriately in her instruction to ensure learning. But in her internship, she had become aware that her professional teammates tended to give some students easier work than seemed appropriate. These were learners who could demonstrate resistance and had low tolerance for frustration. This observation made her feel anxious when she offered more appropriately challenging content. But, she added, she felt a responsibility to be accountable for her students' growth and learning.

This reflection highlighted this candidate's ability to be present to the anxiety she experienced as she noticed a difference between her professional beliefs, and those of teammates, related to providing appropriate levels of challenge to ensure learning. While her perceptions were that her teammates under-challenged some students academically to avoid behavior problems, she chose to allow the discomfort, adhering to her belief about appropriately challenging learners to support growth. She trusted her past experience in courses and earlier part-time field experiences (for both literacy and behavior methods placements) as she remained connected to her new professional knowledge. She noted that her mentors / teammates in her full-time internship appeared to make different decisions, limiting academic challenges, perhaps to avoid difficult student behaviors. Though it made her feel nervous, she chose to trust her own professional knowledge and commitment to accountability for student learning.

Another candidate wrote about how she was able to remain relatively present during co-taught math lessons within her team, and effective in teaching students with disabilities who needed differentiation of instruction. She reported that she felt very confident with the curriculum, and that this supported her to be "there." She stated that, because of her knowledge of the content, she felt more present and conscious of her interactions with students during these lessons. She referred to experiences in which she felt that strategies to support students and also challenge their thinking just "came to her." She also stated that when she did not completely agree with her partner's format for these lessons, she would take a breath, and this would enable her to engage.

This candidate noticed how her professional knowledge (e.g., confidence with the material, the math curriculum) supported her ability to focus on her mindfulness of teaching interactions with students. She also acknowledged that not everything about the conditions was perfect. She did not agree with some of the lesson formats but had little power as an intern. Rather than resist, she took a few breaths and moved on to working with students. She let go of what was contrary to her own preferences and outside of her own control and chose to bring her focus to a part she cares deeply about and can impact: her students. This was a seemingly small, but very mindful choice that could support the development of a healthy response pattern to the complex experiences of co-teaching.

One intern described her experience conducting individual reading assessments for some students she would soon be teaching. Skills were at much lower levels than anticipated. One of the students sometimes presented challenging behaviors, resisting many academic activities. The intern reported how she had noticed that her teammates often did not challenge this student, perhaps to limit the reactivity. She discussed how he did indeed resist during her individual assessment, but she "decided to stay present." She wrote that she remained engaged and supportive and was able to get him to complete the assessment, and that she felt good about this. She discussed that she was anticipating that he might bring some challenges to the group with resistant or distracting behaviors. As his assessments revealed that he had significant learning needs as a reader, she restated her commitment to helping him grow as a reader. Additionally, she reported that she was already considering how to build in some preventative strategies for possible behaviors to support his participation and success.

This candidate shared examples of "choosing presence" during an assessment of a challenging student. She realized from her data that there would likely be significant academic and behavioral challenges when she assumed teaching responsibilities for the small group that included this student. Mindfulness helped her to own the stress that was emerging about this learner's challenging behaviors. Her mindful response was to be proactive about applying her professional knowledge to consider behavior support strategies that might reduce or prevent the difficult behaviors and to be proactive and incorporate these into her instructional planning for the reading group. She was aware of her stress, its source, and about her professional knowledge and intentions. She planned to address her stress by applying professional knowledge and strategies for supporting students who demonstrated difficult behaviors. She was willing to stay present to working with the student's behaviors as a necessary part of her instruction, to help him move him forward as a reader. Key elements supporting her intention and her experiments with mindful teaching included her strong foundation in teaching emergent and early readers, and tools for proactive behavior supports.

A different intern discussed her new responsibility for small group reading instruction. This group included students with multiple reading goals, including phonemic awareness, phonics, and reading continuous texts. The time allotted for this instruction was shorter than her tutoring experience, and she felt anxious about her ability to teach multiple focused activities during this time. She described how she engaged with mental self-talk, reminding herself not to rush. She mentioned reminding herself that she wanted the instruction to be meaningful to support student learning each day, not just to get through activities. She reported feeling better about her increasing presence and her ability to let little things go, to support both academic and behavioral learning for her students.

This candidate was aware that time constraints created stress and reduced her mindfulness during instruction. She made some lesson plan adjustments to thoughtfully reduce the number of learning activities, and did some internal "self-talk" to manage the temptation to "rush" through the lesson so she could stay focused on priorities. In addition to considering how to be more mindful, she was also clear that student learning priorities (academic and behavioral) were central to her efforts.

Inner Experiences: Cultivating Awareness and Skillful Responses

Some comments revealed candidates' growing awareness of their inner experience. These examples described how being more tuned in to body, thoughts, and emotions was related to mindfulness and teaching.

I am getting better about practicing almost every morning. I find on those days when I am not practicing, I notice myself thinking about all the other things I have to do rather than being present to myself or the kids. I tend to be thinking ahead about what I have to do next, what else I have to accomplish. That has been a real challenge for me.

***

I am learning how to take hold of my mind and to observe. I pay more attention to my emotions and sensations and thoughts. But not judging whatever is coming up; just being with it. I am learning to recognize them and go back to myself and breathe. For example, I have become a lot more aware of how I respond to students. This semester I worked with a student who was having a difficult time. He presents a lot of challenging behaviors that are related to his disability. I had to become aware of exactly what I was saying, how I was phrasing it, the tone of my voice, my body language. I really feel like my mindfulness practice helped me in being more present with him and being successful. We could prevent a lot of difficult behaviors.

It's interesting to note that what this teacher is really describing is about being mindful of herself — her words, her tone, her body language. The foundation for this ability to stay connected to herself began in the beginning weeks of practice with mindful teaching, when she tried to notice anxiety and became aware of her typical responses. Through practice, she learned to tolerate the discomfort. Over time she saw how her anxiety could shape her words, her tone, her body language. It felt awkward at first to stay present and experiment with new ways of being in the interaction. Mindfulness was not always comfortable, but it was the root of growing these capacities to teach in challenging moments.

We can bring mindfulness not only during a challenging moment, but in reflecting on the experience after as well.

> *My work is to provide behavioral intervention supports for students who have disabilities. After a difficult student episode, I sometimes try to take a short break somewhere else as soon as conditions allow. First, I just breathe and settle. Then I try to run through the event in my mind and try to examine it, without the emotions. And I will ask myself, "What triggered this behavior for this student? What can I change next time? Is there someone I can talk to about it?" When I try to look back to explore it from a fact-based view, that helps me to understand more. I replay the experience, but it's not like I am obsessing over it and caught in the emotions that came up.*

This teacher is aware of the emotions and thoughts that can come up for her when a student's challenging behaviors escalate. This clouds her ability to understand what is going on. Later, she cultivates mindfulness as she revisits the event. First, she takes care of her emotions by breathing and calming. Only then does she recall and re-examine the situation with the eyes of awareness — to strip it down to what was observable and try to focus on what actually happened in those moments. This can sometimes offer insights that bring more understanding and effective practices to help the student develop new behaviors, a priority learning goal.

> *When one of my students who has a disability presents strong challenging behaviors, I may feel annoyed or disappointed. My body speeds up inside and is like on fast forward. I feel myself tensing up a lot. I always feel it first in my fingertips or my toes. They will curl up when I'm frustrated. A headache begins to come up; I can feel myself getting tense and anxious. When I notice these changes in my body, I know I need to practice and*

> *take care of myself in that moment. It helps me if I take one or two steps back and maybe glance out the window while I focus on breathing. That little bit of physical space and visual change in scenery helps me to disconnect from the fear, soothe myself and breathe it out.*

This teacher, who supports interventions for students who sometimes have very difficult behaviors, had shared how this body awareness continued to evolve in her practice after a couple of years. With practice, mindfulness of the body can help us to notice strong emotions and remember to practice with these before we become overwhelmed. One of the major themes that candidates share about their graduate school lives, and their lives in general, is the suffering they experience from anxiety. Rachel's reflection at the end of her first graduate semester (below) described how mindfulness practices offered benefits to her for being present to and managing her anxiety in her teaching, and now across life experiences.

> *When I received an email this summer that explained a few requirements for this class, I was completely overcome with anxiety, and the class had not even started yet. I have been battling anxiety for as long as I can remember and have the tendency to end up physically ill over things that I have no control over. To be honest, I felt very skeptical that being mindful would really have an impact on me. As life would have it, I was proved wrong.*
>
> *Learning about mindfulness is what helped me the most this semester. Driving my car gives me so much time to think and obsess about things that may never happen. (My mother calls this worst-case scenario thinking.) I find when I get to my destination, I am upset without a good reason why. In the comfort of my car and parking lots, I began taking time before I got out of my car to be mindful. I would turn the radio off,*

rest my head back, and simply breathe and be in the moment. Sometimes it would be for one minute, sometimes it was for 10 minutes. I found that I did not have to hold on to the negative emotions and feelings I had just stepped away from because they weren't anything I really needed to worry about anyway. It was a revelation that I could feel so good at 7 am on a Monday morning.

Breathing and being mindful in the car before I got out helped with tutoring Nicholas. Even if I had a bad day, I would have a second wave of energy that I was ready to focus on Nicholas and teaching. Being mindful has helped me enjoy life. I overall feel happier right now than I have in a while. I wake up in the morning and I feel thankful. I feel happy. I feel more. In my household, having feelings is not always welcome. We tend to view feelings as unnecessary and even a nuisance to have. Becoming mindful gave me permission to feel emotions, something even a counselor could not help me with in the past. Sadness is always an emotion that people want to fix and stop. I have found when I take time to truly feel my sadness, I am able to move on quicker. I do not feel the need to dwell on it anymore. After I take time to feel, I can focus on how I am going to proceed and live my next moments.

My response to Rachel:

Thank you so much for sharing so richly about your experiments and experiences with mindfulness. This is why I must share these practices — I think that no matter how much we "know," unless we are mindful, our impact as teachers will not necessarily be the most effective or reflect our best offering. You express so many understandings so well. You have developed an authentic practice and are very intentional. You are able to observe your body and feelings and mind — which is fundamental — and use mindfulness skillfully to support your decision making. I have witnessed your steadiness grow throughout the semester, and with it, your confidence. Mindfulness practice can help us to access our true self – where we are all powerful and worthwhile. This is, of course, the self we want to share with ourselves and others. I so appreciate this reflection. I hope and trust you will continue to grow your practice.

Intention as a Vision and a Compass

Intention, a theme that had emerged from many documents about my mindful teaching, was also present in multiple candidate reflections. Though not explicitly named, I noted stories candidates shared in which they made decisions that honored their intention as educators.

One intern wrote about a student who had begun presenting behavioral challenges during small group reading. He stated that he had talked about participation expectations before the first lesson but had not made a visual written copy. He wrote that he also realized now that he did not provide a visual schedule of the lesson parts and sequence either. He described how the student's behaviors were creating frequent interruptions and how he found himself constantly addressing her. He went on to write that he had become aware how he had really lost his presence with this group. He admitted that he was losing confidence.

He went on to write that in the past week, he had made some changes. He had written out behavioral expectation reminders and reviewed these briefly before each lesson. He described how sometimes he was able to point to the chart and use non-verbal cues when this individual student began getting distracted. Sometimes this was enough redirection. He also developed a simple visual schedule with the order of the lesson's parts to review each day. He wrote that by the end of the week, this group felt completely different. He said that he felt like he was teaching again and their transitions between activities were going much better. He went on to write that, at one point, his challenging student got up and left the table. He explained how he went to her and talked quietly. He took a deep breath before he spoke and remained calm as he invited her back to read. She returned to the table. He went on to report that she was actually more engaged and confident for the rest of that lesson. He described how he felt the whole lesson was impacted by his mindfulness in that small moment, as he stayed calm and invited her back. He cited this as an example of how relationships are important in supporting teaching and learning. He stated that he would continue to try to build his relationships with all of his students.

This intern understood that, after a disappointing start with this group, he had not met his intention. He realized and adjusted, aware that being present or mindful as a teacher includes thorough preparation beforehand and taking responsibility for facilitating. In hindsight, he was aware that his plans did not include some known strategies and materials to support student engagement, and that he allowed the student's behaviors to control the lesson. His mindful response was to revise plans with a focus on his intention to be present as the teacher he wants to be and to maximize student learning. This preparation for the second lesson supported the group's success and his ability to have a skillful and mindful interaction "in the moment" with a student. His attention to relationships with his students addressed his intention as well, directed by his consciousness of who he wants to be as a teacher.

During this semester I went through a frustrating relationship breakup. It happened an hour before I needed to be at school for tutoring. This was a true test of being mindful. Nicholas deserves me at my best so he can become his best. I took longer in the car to breathe before I came in. While tutoring, I focused on what Nicholas did and said harder than I ever had before in an attempt to be present with him and not let my thoughts suffocate me. I was relieved when Nicholas left the building, but I felt like I succeeded. This was a life-changing moment for me. I was able to overcome the anxiety for the hour I needed to most.

This reflection captures this graduate student's clarity about her professional intention to meet her aspiration, even when experiencing her own very strong challenging emotions. She was able to choose presence for her student and to provide her best teaching offering for this lesson.

There was a week I was so overwhelmed, and I just didn't practice. I could feel things getting frazzled, things were not going well. It seemed there were a lot more difficult behaviors. I was annoyed. And I went home at the end of the week and said to myself, "What are you doing? This is not you." And the next week I decided to start practicing every day again at home — and I started going to my car at lunchtime. I knew I needed to practice. The next week wasn't perfect, but it was so much better. I found myself calmer, introducing more preventatives for some behaviors, getting into a teaching routine again. I really notice when I don't practice every day. It's cool when you see the benefit — but if you stop it's not cool, and you notice.

This individual's difficulties prompted her to look inward, and to ask herself, "What are you doing?" She recognized, "This is not you." The frustration brought her back to, "Who do I want to be as a teacher?" She also cites how her mindfulness practice creates the conditions for her to teach with intention. And it was her awareness, her growing mindfulness of her intention, that made her notice her offering was not aligned with her intention that week.

I have a student labeled as having Oppositional Defiant Disorder. He really likes control and controlling situations. Since I have been practicing more daily, I find myself thinking more carefully about the language I use with him. In our conversations, I am able to pause and reflect in the moment on what I want to say to him before I said it. He is responding so much better. When I reacted and just said the first thing that came to mind, he would always get control and demand things. But in our relationship now, I am able to pause and take a step back and think a little bit, and that was because I was able to be present with him. I am better able to help him be stable and keep myself stable as well. I credit that to being able to be present in the moment.

This reflection illustrates how this candidate's intention helped her focus on presence, relationship, and using careful, skillful speech with a complicated student. Her stability creates conditions for this student to experience more stability. This supports his engagement, participation, and learning in both his academic and social-emotional goals.

The above candidate examples highlight wholesome dispositions. These reflections demonstrate a clear commitment to authentic learning and accountability for student progress. Many stories also illustrate respect and caring for all students, and attention to social-emotional learning – for learners who present the most difficulty. This orientation to their teaching work, connected to decisions, small and large, captures moments of advocacy in action, and engaged practice.

Heartened by the Unexpected

I was surprised and encouraged by many of the reflections candidates wrote about during the full-time internship semester. For the vast majority, the internship was completed a year after their initial semester when they completed the literacy course and field experience. As previously mentioned, no instruction or coaching in mindfulness or mindful teaching had been offered since the end of their first graduate semester (a period of nine months). As part of the seminar that accompanied the internship, candidates were prompted to write a bit each week about teaching related experiences during their placements. Writing prompts included a general prompt about mindfulness of their experience (i.e., "a time when you felt you were mindful of your experience" or "a time when you realized you were not mindful and what you might have done differently"). One surprise was the thoughtful and well-developed responses that were offered related to the mindfulness prompt. I was not expecting this almost a year after our shared experience in the literacy block. Many were detailed, honest and often quite vulnerable. Equally affirming were how disappointments often included actions or plans to respond to difficulties in ways that integrated mindfulness practices with skills and strategies from their coursework and prior field experiences.

For me, the most powerful elements of many of the candidates' reflections during their internship were their clarity and courage. Here is why I am deeply touched by stories that reflect their sense of commitment and agency, especially in these conditions.

I can recall my full-time student teaching semester in my initial teacher preparation program. There were two eight-week placements. I (and I believe everyone I knew from the program) blindly adopted and implemented the practices of my mentor teacher. The faculty who (occasionally) visited to observe never questioned this, nor did they encourage me to bring a critical lens to practices or to have agency in my decision making. Unfortunately, I have witnessed that this kind of capstone field experience continues in many teacher-preparation programs and remains unquestioned.

I know that joining a team as an unpaid intern / student teacher from a university program (undergraduate or graduate) is an extremely powerless position. Our small graduate program supported "best educational practices," and we expected our candidates' decisions to include and reflect what we had offered them during their studies in this respect. As full-time faculty, we supervised and coached them in these placements. We did our best to choose high quality teacher partners for our placements. But even in our best placement, there were elements that were not consistent with best practices for some learners. Our candidates were also required to provide some instruction in general education classrooms, co-teaching with a general education partner who was not their mentor. Here the quality of classroom practices for learners with disabilities was sometimes not the best. The demands of this internship experience were high (as they are in the professional role they were pursuing).

A number of our candidates discussed situations where their professional teammates' practices did not match their own perceptions of appropriate professional decision making. These realities challenged them to "remember what they knew and believed." And, often, they did. They responded in small ways — and sometimes not so small ways — with integrity. They reported a lot of anxiety but stayed connected to their true teacher selves. They were not judgmental of their teammates and did their best to share different ideas skillfully.

This is the power of mindfulness. These inexperienced, anxious — and well-prepared, very capable — candidates were, at least sometimes, able to be mindful about the very challenging conditions of this work. They could reflect on a tough lesson or challenging context with mindfulness, without blame or shame. They often responded with ways to stop and calm and care for themselves. Then they were able to look deeply and take responsibility for their teaching or teaming, finding they had more to offer to support conditions for learners' success.

They reported and reflected on instances where they chose mindfulness and did not "cave" to their anxiety.

This ability to stay present to one's individual experience and take responsibility for one's self — and the conditions we can shape — is powerful. I believe the foundation for just and healthy educational systems rests on individual teachers who are clear about their intention and can tolerate the discomfort that inevitably comes with ethical decision making. This is why I am heartened by what I read in so many candidate reflections.

Chapter 12
Reflections on the Journey

My long journey in pursuit of mindful teaching included unexpected joys, as well as suffering and confusion. All of these experiences eventually yielded insights. The path does not end. These mind states still visit as I practice in new teaching and learning contexts.

Early unplanned experiences (with Damien, Misha) watered seeds of my aspiration to bring a focus on mindfulness into my work as an educator. I became curious about the elements that supported mindfulness in my teaching, and how I might cultivate these. As discussed in preceding chapters, three major insights emerged from my exploration of mindful teaching. These are attention to: (a) my professional knowledge, skills, and dispositions; (b) my inner experience (physical, emotional, thoughts); and (c) my intention.

Awareness of each of these three elements seems to create the best conditions for me to bring more mindfulness to this complex work. If mindful teaching is the seed of my aspiration, then awareness of my professional knowledge and skills, of my inner experience, and of my intention are the soil, the water, and the sunlight that can help it to manifest. Like the gardener, my ability to tend to each of these conditions can support my seed of mindful teaching to grow strong and steady through the seasons of my teaching life. I recognize now how these three conditions are deeply interconnected as they support my aspiration of mindful teaching. Each may develop at different times and rates. For example, my long and deep experience in my professional learning came long before my mindfulness practice. Yet even my very early attention to mindfulness as an inexperienced practitioner had a powerful impact on my teaching with Damien. Similarly, just beginning to reflect on and clarify my intention had a tremendous effect when combined with professional knowledge and a beginning mindfulness practice, with Damien, Kiera, and some adult learners. The absence of my wholesome intention seemed to be the barrier to my success with Misha (and with some adult learners).

I observed similar influences with my graduate students who were pre-service special educators, just beginning to grow their professional knowledge and skills in this complex field. Nearly all of them were new to mindfulness practice, introduced to it in small bites for the first time in my classes while they were engaged in rigorous professional development. I shared the idea of articulating my intention just a bit to the last few years of candidates, as it emerged in my own exploration. Yet these busy, beginning, not yet certified professionals, who were very inexperienced mindfulness practitioners with just some exposure to intention, recognized and shared many moments of mindful teaching. Perhaps like the soil and water and sunshine, "good enough" conditions can be sufficient to touch mindfulness in our teaching. My own experience and my observations suggest that with even beginning awareness of each of these conditions, mindful teaching can begin to emerge.

My teaching work can be complex, and much of it is dynamic and unscripted. It includes many interactions and decisions through changing conditions. I wondered how I might begin to bring awareness from my foundational practice into the realities of my actual day to day teaching. I was not clear on how to invite this gentle awareness from my quiet personal practice into my teaching. Even as I became a more experienced practitioner, I often struggled to maintain mindfulness in my work.

The following are some insights about what has been helpful to me.

Cultivating and sustaining a daily mindfulness practice is critical, but not the whole story. It seems that my personal and teaching practice are in an ongoing dance. My foundational practice provides stability, at least as a starting point each day. It helps me to integrate basic tools that might be easily accessed during the day to nourish or recover (e.g., breath). Additionally, noticing patterns of success and challenge in my teaching life helps me to choose where I might focus my daily practice. For a long time, my daily practice was to follow my breath to quiet and calm. I am learning that my capacity for mindful teaching benefits from additional practices to support specific kinds of challenges my patterns bump into. For me, this includes my habitual reactivity, which can charge my speech patterns and energy in ways that create anxiety in and disconnection from my students and others. Similarly, my sometimes-strong attachment to particular outcomes and processes can create a lot of anxiety for me that limits my decisions and interactions. To support my ability to manage (and maybe someday transform) these patterns, it continues to be important for me to focus regularly on practices related to body sensations, strong emotions, and unwholesome thoughts. Though not reported in these explorations, my more recent opportunities to learn more about my zone of resilience, and how to track, nourish, and regulate my nervous system (Rosen, 2023; Ward, n.d.) remain extremely helpful. These understandings help me to recognize and practice with some of my habitual patterns that do not support mindfulness in my teaching and other spheres of my life. The dance between my practice and my teaching experience is ongoing, with each informing and supporting the other.

Another important lesson for me has been the power of articulating and staying in touch with my intention. Reflecting on my teaching ancestors, and envisioning what shapes my offering, helps to ground me in my best teacher-self. Even gentle awareness of this element seems to strengthen my consciousness of when I am facing the right direction — the one that aligns with my intention. It also often helps me to recognize when my thinking or actions go astray, so that I can re-orient. For me, intention is a touchstone that supports my ability to pursue my aspiration for my teaching to be a noble offering.

One more aspect that I have found to be supportive of my mindfulness in teaching is to try to tune in to my energies of power and vulnerability. When I can be in touch with my vulnerability, as well as my very real strengths, it supports my conditions for mindfulness. Allowing vulnerability for me may take the form of not over-planning for a class or workshop, or scripting what I will say in a meeting with someone. It means letting go of some of my control and trusting my ability to participate as things unfold with "just enough" preparation. Sometimes, before a big presentation or a challenging meeting, I will meditate to bring myself back to an experience of tenderness with a trusted friend or mentor, or a time when I "got this right." Often when I do this, my muscles relax, my heart softens, tears may well up. My energy shifts, allowing space for compassion and connection, as well as competence. I know other individuals whose tendency is to underestimate their capacity and feel anxiety or fear. They report that this impedes their ability to teach with mindfulness. Maybe for these individuals, the opposite is needed: to practice getting in touch with a time when they were indeed powerful and successful and to own and feel their strength.

I have tried to find words for many aspects of my journey in search of mindful teaching. One of the great gifts of this exploration for me has been the "felt sense" of mindful teaching that I have experienced in small moments, as well as some longer classes and sessions. My first and most powerful teacher, the one who set me on this path of inquiry, was a 12-year-old boy whom few people even considered to be a capable learner. The following is an excerpt from my journal, reflecting on my time with Damien, noting my awareness of our unique experience.

But I am also aware of something else. I am really enjoying him. I realize that I am relaxed and in the flow. I am leading, structuring, facilitating; but also reading him and responding. I am really experimenting, not knowing what he will do with what I present, knowing it's possible that he may not care, or try, not knowing if he will need help or how much or if I will be able to figure out how to support him. I am subtly aware of these possibilities, but I don't dwell there. I don't get anxious or stuck or try to force anything, or direct or control things. He, I suspect, is coming from a similar place. He does not know me either, or what I have, or what I will share or ask of him. But he is curious, too, and open. He does not resist. He is willing to go there with me, to explore a little bit.

He is mostly responding, but more than once, he definitely initiates, to take the mouse, to drop the mouse and reach for the keys, to sign to me when we finish one sentence and then two, "More ... more...." There is some very real energy here, flowing between us in both directions.

I try to remember the last time my teaching felt so authentic, so right.

My time with Damien offered me an embodied experience of mindful teaching and inspired me to cultivate my capacity to be *this* teacher for *"more ... more..."* of my teaching days.

Lessons from My Beginning Teacher Candidates

The opportunity to invite and support my graduate students to join this experiment enriched and deepened my learning. Their efforts and reflections about bringing mindfulness into their lives and their teaching encouraged my own practice and supported emerging insights. I was often struck and humbled by what they shared, aware that they were so early on their paths as both educators and mindfulness practitioners. They helped me to understand that benefits can begin to develop early in our practice, and that even only occasional moments of success can encourage and empower us.

While there was variation in how much individuals engaged with this mindful teaching exploration, the vast majority described meaningful experiences while in the graduate program. Nearly all were brand new to mindfulness practice. Some of their most valuable lessons described their beginning mindfulness practice and the conditions that supported their first steps on the path.

Introducing Mindfulness and Supporting Early Practice

Before I began introducing mindfulness practices to my candidates, I had been actively cultivating my own practice and learning from teachers, from retreats, from teacher mentors and from my fellow practitioners with whom I met weekly to practice together. I was conscious of what had been helpful to me, and this informed what I shared, and how I did so. As described in chapter seven, my introductory experiences grew over several years. Many of the comments below refer to later years when I offered my direct guidance and support for their practice. I focused mostly on facilitating brief guided experiences with a variety of practices, and then inviting individuals to notice their experience. I emphasized that there was no right or wrong response, that different individuals may experience the same practice quite differently. The encouragement was to tune in to one's own experience.

> *I liked that you introduced it in many ways. We did the mindful walking. And I used to just think about that when I was walking from class to class. It was very practical. We even did mindful eating – we ate some chocolate mindfully! I remember that – and sometimes I do it at lunch. ... I was never taught that mindfulness was something that we could do in daily life. That was news. I remember being amazed at how calming the walking meditation was. I had never experienced anything like that and did not realize how effective that could be. Up until that time I thought that meditation was only the traditional sitting. This class was*

> *my first real introduction to mindfulness and to different kinds of meditation.*

I began to make a few explicit connections to potential benefits of mindfulness for teachers and share some research on education related mindfulness studies.

> *The way you introduced it was so practical and we could really see how it applies to our teaching. Like in our daily decision making during our reading tutoring lessons.*
>
> *For me, it was helpful to read some articles ... about research behind it that shows how this is powerful and how it can help you in your everyday life and in teaching. It definitely made me want to explore more and to keep trying.... Learning about the mind encourages me to practice more. Knowing how this can benefit me makes me want to practice more. It affects me and all around me and how I participate in life.*

Though I encouraged trying out a brief daily practice, it became clear that no one did so after the first introduction. (I would have them write to me anonymously after a couple weeks to say if they had engaged in any further practice.) I added more support for practice and feedback. The next semester I "required" candidates to practice for at least 5 minutes a day five days of the week following the intro to practice class. The introduction had included following some guided practice on free apps. They were invited to practice with or without these tools. After each day's short practice, they were invited to write briefly (a paragraph) about their experience for that session. We used an online classroom managements system (Blackboard), so I could see the date when they posted each of their comments. This was an ungraded activity with no rewards or sanctions. But their positive energy about a new semester resulted in every person participating. They engaged with daily or almost daily practice that week. They noticed and wrote about their experience. I intentionally did not respond to any of their postings until the next week. I wanted each of them to own their experiment and observations, and not shape them to my feedback. At the end of the week, I wrote feedback about their observations and encouraged them to continue.

> *And there was a follow through, which for me is what helped. Anyone can introduce you to something, but if they are not showing genuine interest you may not really try it. Having the (ungraded) assignment to practice on our own the first week and write just a little reflection each time, that definitely helped me to explore a little more. It wasn't like practice one time. It was a nice task for me and a challenge to try every day.*

***

> *I love the apps and choosing guided meditations. I love the visualizations. A body scan is my favorite, my go-to for everything. It allows me to surrender to that moment. I just feel like I am noticing more, like more self-awareness. I can focus and I know I can do that.*

***

> *On the third day of that first week (of assigned practice), I thought I would not need a guided meditation, and that I could just do one with just a timer bell for 10 minutes. I remember feeling how difficult it was and just being like totally mindful of that. It was not that simple. It was going to be something that I would have to work at. Because I did enjoy how clear my mind would feel after, it was something I wanted to go after and try.*

I had also encouraged candidates to practice for even a few minutes before their transition to tutoring and graduate class.

Most were working in schools as daily substitute teachers and traveled directly to the tutoring site. I decided in the last few years to meet as a group before they met their individual students. We practiced together as I guided a 5-minute meditation of breath and body. Then I would try to send them off with a smile and some freshness.

> *I see how you helped us practice it. The first week on our own, and then the fact that we all did a guided meditation together with you week after week, every Monday and Tuesday, before every tutoring session. It made me recognize it might only take a couple of minutes but could really be incorporated into our routine and schedule. And it could bring so much benefit.*

***

> *That first semester I would not have meditated before every tutoring session if we had not done it together. I found that to be so helpful. I definitely had days where I was stuck in traffic or was late or already my mind was running and scrambled. I think it allowed like a grounding sense to return to my zone. I could go into tutoring with a fresh mind, instead of the chaotic energy I walked in with. It definitely helped a lot.*

Some students noted and reflected on how their practice varied and changed, and how they noticed or pursued benefits beyond our class.

> *It was cool because I found myself in grad school getting lost in my work. I am an overachiever. I like getting things done. I like getting good grades ... and you really lose yourself if you have that mentality. It was nice to take that (practice) time for myself and remind myself that you have to take care of yourself too when all the busyness arises.*

***

I noticed that it is not the same every time I practice. I was more scattered at first, but when it became a daily routine, I saw the benefit — big picture — but not necessarily every single time I practiced. That's when I really began to notice the benefits in my teaching and my life.

***

In addition to morning practice, I started to listen to this playlist, called "Mindfulness for Anxiety." That has really helped me to be more present in everyday life and to transform my teaching. I would do it in the morning — or when I had a big homework or planning day, I would have that on in the background. It kept me calm and it kept me really focused. It starts off with a guided meditation — then there are just nature sounds like rainfall or instrumental music. I feel like I am not worrying as much or questioning myself all the time.

***

A huge part of it for me was learning to be nonjudgmental toward myself with my practice. I definitely was judging myself a lot in the beginning. I would get mad at myself. Why couldn't I focus? What was I doing wrong? A lot of just anger at myself for not being able to be in the moment. I found it very easy to get frustrated with myself when my mind was wandering during practice or when I felt I was unsuccessful. Those judgments. But then I learned to recognize it as it is and go back to what I knew how to do: Breathe.

Although this introduction to mindfulness represented just a fraction of our course content and class time, some adopted and sustained a daily practice, and described significant benefits in their lives, as well as their teaching. Rachel, for example, wrote:

> *I feel that being mindful will, and already has, made me a better teacher. Instead of taking things children do personally, I am able to take a step back and think. Reacting is easy and I am guilty of still doing it. More often, I am able to have a mindful response. I feel I am a calmer presence in the room than I have been in the past. I look forward to having my own classroom someday and teaching my students to be mindful as well. I think it will be one of my top behavior management methods. I wonder how different my life would be if I had learned mindful techniques in elementary school. Being mindful is not just meditation; it is a way of life. I am incredibly blessed that I had the opportunity to be exposed to and to practice being mindful this semester. I will take what I learned and apply it to the rest of my life.*

Leah's final first semester reflection went even deeper:

> *Looking back at this past August I feel as if I have grown as an individual. I entered this graduate program nervous and scared that I may fail. I remember leaving the first class feeling like I was not going to make it through this semester. My self-doubt was at an all-time high. Undergrad was the best and worst times of my life. When I graduated in May I felt this overwhelming feeling of disappointment in myself, and it wasn't until this semester that I have been able to pinpoint the source of this feeling. While I walked across that stage in honor society and cum laude sashes, I thought more about the times I had skipped class rather than the proud achievements I had displayed upon my gown.*
>
> *When I returned home for the summer and attended the graduation parties of my hometown friends, something still*

didn't feel right for me. Everyone around me seemed to have their lives together and I just couldn't share in that moment. Over the course of the summer months, I constantly compared myself to my successful friends around me. I couldn't help but feel that I was less than them. Most of my friends bragged of their big-time job offers and plans to move to cities, while the others were happily planning their weddings. I, on the other hand, was returning to my undergrad college to go to the same school where I had just spent four years. Four years where my main concerns were what bar to go to at night and what fast food to consume the next day. Needless to say, I was very hesitant when the semester start date rolled around, as I was nervous to land in the same old bad habits I had acquired in undergrad. It is also essential that I say that, after leaving my first day of classes in this program, I felt so much more on track to start my adult life.

While I may not be making a great salary or planning out my life with a significant other beside me, I have never felt more confident in my life. Ever since you introduced me to the practice of mindfulness, I have taken back control of my life. I could not be more confident that returning to this college for graduate school was the right step for me. My mindfulness app is the most used app on my phone, and I believe is a huge component in this self-acceptance journey I am on. I never thought taking a step back from this hectic world we live in would actually have such a profound impact on me. My daily mindfulness meditations make me feel like I am in power. I am learning more about me each and every day. I think the most important thing I've learned throughout this practice is that mindfulness doesn't always bring the good. Mindfulness makes you aware of your problems and escapes. Simply acknowledging this has really helped me grow as a student, a teacher, and an individual.

The nervousness I used to feel before teaching a lesson is so much less than it used to be. I am no longer scared to mess up my instruction, because I know if I do, I can adjust. I know I have the knowledge and tools to be successful; it is just now that I am finally putting them to use. Instead of getting flustered and forgetting what I've been taught, I have learned to respond to situations rather than react to them. This is one of the greatest life lessons I have become aware of. In my tutoring sessions, I am easily thrown off by Nathan's behavior on certain days. He can be very distracted and it used to take a toll on me. I would blame it on myself or get so frustrated that I would lose focus of the lesson objectives. I now find it much more helpful to try and breathe in the moment and recognize what is happening. I find myself spontaneously offering suggestions to him like stretching or the choice to stand up for some activities. I realize that he is a child that just sat through a full school day and is now sitting through an hour of reading instruction. I find myself constantly reflecting on our sessions together. Without even noticing it, I automatically review my lesson outline and can pinpoint areas where I could have been more engaging with him. I am constantly seeking to better our lessons.

I am also pleased to see that I am not the only one doing so. It is a relief to have such a class with open-minded individuals. I feel welcome to share my experiences with my classmates. I have never had an issue with being social with my classmates before, but the conversations I have with this group are so much more meaningful. I see the value in the chats we have as I catch myself wanting to help others out. Being mindful allows me to take a step back from my ego and be honest with people. I see someone struggling and I do not feel ashamed to admit to the same struggles. More importantly, I feel motivated to come up with a solution together. In the past I would bottle up any / all problems I encountered during class time and find myself with a mental breakdown. I have found that something as simple as a daily-guided meditation can profoundly impact my mental health. This is not to say I live a stress-free life

> *now but accepting that stress is there is so much better than pretending it is not. Being present can be uncomfortable at times, but it allows me to break old habits and focus on what is best for me. I see this change in my everyday life, whether I am the teacher, the student, or the 22-year-old girl.*

Both candidates shared these reflections at the end of their first semester in the program, only 12 weeks after being introduced to mindfulness practices. We all need to find our own stability and trust our foundation. Honest and tender responses of this kind affirmed that mindfulness was perhaps my most meaningful offering.

Parting Thoughts

This book is a deep reflection of my journey to understand and cultivate mindfulness in my teaching life. I offered stories about some of the people and experiences that invited and supported my learning. But let me be the first to admit that I am often not the mindful person who is represented in some of the stories shared here. I am still, more often than I'd like, irritable, impatient, and judgmental. There are times that I talk too much and don't listen with my full attention. The mindful life can be humbling. Many of my unskillful habit energies (which were transmitted from a long line of ancestors with remarkably similar characteristics) will always be with me.

The difference now is that, for a few more moments on many days, I am present to my experience and that of others. I can respond sometimes instead of reacting. I can notice a need, and sometimes, offer my presence and support, even if only for a few moments of connection. And, gratefully, I am much more likely to notice when I have been inattentive or unkind or less than present. I can take steps to begin anew. My progress is reflected not in that my negative behaviors have been extinguished, but in that they are less frequent or intense, and I notice sooner. I am more quickly able to recognize my unskillfulness, without blaming others, and without judging or rejecting parts of myself. I am more conscious of positive and skillful traits and possibilities in myself and others, and to practice ways to cultivate these, so that they might be a more frequent part of my offering.

Mindfulness is a journey and a way of life each day, not a destination or an outcome. I know now that it is about being connected to all of my characteristics and experiences, without harsh judgment or pride. The more I am able to accept my limitations and recognize my setbacks on my teaching path, the more I can connect fully with my more wholesome possibilities – which is fundamental to being open to the possibilities in others.

What I have shared in these pages is my experience and the insights that have emerged in the last decade of a lifetime of teaching. If some of these insights resonate with you or inspire you, I hope they might be of benefit on your teaching journey. For anything here that does not ring true, please let it go, and stay open to what is presenting and calling for attention on your path.

About the Author

Roberta F. Schnorr, Ph.D. served as a professional educator for over forty years. This included nine years teaching in K-12 public schools and over twenty years as coordinator of a graduate teacher preparation program at State University of New York at Oswego. She is a founding member and co-leader of the Apple Blossom Sangha which practices in the Plum Village Buddhist tradition. In 2016 she became a member of the Plum Village Order of Interbeing. She lives in Central New York where she enjoys reading, writing, silence, authentic conversations, walking, exploring nature, and experiencing all of life's joys and sorrows with family and friends.

References

Brown, Brené (2023, November 14). *Atlas of the Heart List of Emotion.* https://brenebrown.com/resources/ atlas-of-the-heart-list-of-emotions/.

Brown, B. (2012). *Daring Greatly: How the Courage to Be Vulnerable Transforms the Way We Live, Love, Parent and Lead.* New York: Penguin Random House.

Chodron, P. (1997). *When Things Fall Apart: Heart Advice for Difficult Times.* Boston: Shambala Publications.

Figueres, C. (2023, November 20). *Christiana Figueres — Ecological Hope, and Spiritual Evolution.* The On Being Project. https://onbeing.org/programs/christiana-figueres-ecological-hope-and-spiritual-evolution/#transcript.

Friday, J. (2019, April 12–16). Dharma talk from retreat, "Love in Action: Joy on the Path." Springwater Center, Springwater, New York.

Lerner, H. (2017). *Why Won't You Apologize? Healing Big Betrayals and Everyday Hurts.* New York: Gallery Books.

Nhat Hanh, T. (2009). *Happiness: Essential Mindfulness Practices.* Berkeley CA: Parallax Press.

Nhat Hanh, T. (2014). *No Mud, No Lotus: The Art of Transforming Suffering.* Berkeley CA: Parallax Press.

Nhat Hanh, T. (1991). 'Waging Peace,' in *Peace is Every Step* (p.99). New York: Bantam Books.

Nhat Hanh, T. (2021). *Plum Village.* Retrieved January 18, 2024, from https://plumvillage.org/library/clips/what-is-mindfulness.

Rosen, J. (2023). *Unshakeable: Trauma-Informed Mindfulness for Collective Awakening.* Berkely, CA: Parallax Press.

Ward, L. (n.d.). *Deeper Still Academy.* Retrieved January 18, 2024, from https://lotusinstitute.thinkific.com/courses/the-earth-gate#cst-v2-section-x7PGj9LjJO.

MANTRA
BOOKS

EASTERN RELIGION & PHILOSOPHY

We publish books on Eastern religions and philosophies.
Books that aim to inform and explore the various traditions
that began in the East and have migrated West.
If you have enjoyed this book, why not tell other readers by
posting a review on your preferred book site.

Recent Bestsellers from MANTRA BOOKS Are:

The Way Things Are
A Living Approach to Buddhism
Lama Ole Nydahl
An introduction to the teachings of the Buddha, and how to make use of these teachings in everyday life.
Paperback: 978-1-84694-042-2 ebook: 978-1-78099-845-9

Back to the Truth
5000 Years of Advaita
Dennis Waite
A demystifying guide to Advaita for both those new to, and those familiar with this ancient, non-dualist philosophy from India.
Paperback: 978-1-90504-761-1 ebook: 978-184694-624-0

Shinto: A Celebration of Life
Aidan Rankin
Introducing a gentle but powerful spiritual pathway reconnecting humanity with Great Nature and arming all aspects of life.
Paperback: 978-1-84694-438-3 ebook: 978-1-84694-738-4

In the Light of Meditation
Mike George
A comprehensive introduction to the practice of meditation and the spiritual principles behind it. A 10 lesson meditation programme with CD and internet support.
Paperback: 978-1-90381-661-5

The 7 Levels of Wisdom
Mónica Esgueva
A straightforward and compelling approach on how to reach the highest levels of consciousness, wisdom, and inner peace.
Paperback: 978-1-80341-470-6 ebook: 978-1-80341-471-3

Compassion Based Living Course
Heather Regan-Addis and Choden
A practical guide to living a compassionate life.
Paperback: 978-1-80341-676-2 ebook: 978-1-80341-709-7

The Sacred Gathas of Zarathushtra & the Old Avestan Canon
Pablo Vazquez
The ancient and mystical poetry of Zarathushtra and the first Zoroastrians: Now accessible to the public in a modern translation.
Paperback: 978-1-78535-961-3 ebook: 978-1-78535-962-0

Radiant Bliss
Sue Bushell
Embrace Your Journey: Unfolding Peace, Power, and Purpose Through Yoga
Paperback: 978-1-80341-818-6 ebook: 978-1-80341-822-3

Ordinary Women, Extraordinary Wisdom
Rita Marie Robinson
The Feminine Face of Awakening
A collection of intimate conversations with female spiritual teachers who live like ordinary women, but are engaged with their true natures.
Paperback: 978-1-84694-068-2 ebook: 978-1-78099-908-1

The Riddle of Alchemy
Paul Kiritsis
What is alchemy, exactly? Is there any empirical truth to ancient speculative pursuits toward metallic transmutation? How does alchemy intersect with Western mind sciences and science in general?
Paperback: 978-1-80341-637-3 ebook: 978-1-80341-688-5

Readers of ebooks can buy or view any of these bestsellers by clicking on the live link in the title. Most titles are published in paperback and as an ebook. Paperbacks are available in traditional bookshops. Both print and ebook formats are available online.

Find more titles and sign up to our readers' newsletter at www.collectiveinkbooks.com/mind-body-spirit. Follow us on Facebook at facebook.com/OBooks and Twitter at twitter.com/obooks

